KU-485-526

Marie Herbert
GREAT POLAR ADVENTURES

maps by Wally Herbert

cover illustration by Richard Hook

A Piccolo Original

Pan Books London and Sydney

First published 1976 by Pan Books Ltd
Cavaye Place, London SW10 9PG
2nd printing 1976
© Marie Herbert 1976
ISBN 0 330 24625 9
Made and printed in Great Britain by
Cox & Wyman Ltd, London, Reading and Fakenham

Contents

Illustrations

for
Poul Kilt
a great little friend
from Greenland

1 The Arctic explorers

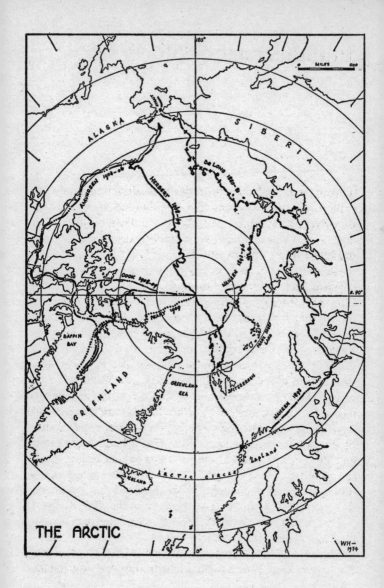

THE ARCTIC

Introduction

The first explorers were primitive men, driven by hunger to explore the world beyond the over-hunted area in which they lived. As the years passed, natural disasters, fear of an enemy, or sheer curiosity continued to draw man beyond the limits of the known world.

Until the Vikings began their sea voyages, most discoveries had been made overland. It was not until the fifteenth century that the 'great age of discovery' dawned, during which the shapes of oceans and continents became mapped out with reasonable accuracy for the first time. Even then there still remained vast uncharted areas around the Poles, and it was not until our own century that man could claim to have reached the ends of the Earth.

The great era of Arctic exploration began in Elizabethan days after the discovery of the Americas. There were several reasons for this, but the most important was the fact that Spain and Portugal controlled the seas around Cape Horn and the Cape of Good Hope; this meant that England ran the gauntlet of two powerful navies when her ships sailed round the world to the east. What she needed was a short, direct and safe route to the treasures of the Orient – and remember that at this time neither the Suez nor the Panama Canal had been cut.

The route seemed obvious – it would have to go north. For over three centuries the battle with the north was to take its toll of men's lives as the attack was pushed along the North-east Passage, the North-west Passage, and across the Pole itself. Explorers drove their ships into great fields of ice where they were battered by storms, blinded by blizzards and often crushed and sunk. All too frequently men met their death racked by starvation and cold.

But through the suffering came success, and with it an example of courage, patience and endurance which we should not easily forget.

Mutiny in the Arctic
Hudson

Not every man who joined the hazardous expeditions to the Arctic was a hero. Sometimes the suffering and hardship was so intolerable that it brought out the worst aspects of a person's character instead of the best.

One of the saddest stories of the early days of Arctic adventure surrounds Henry Hudson. I can remember as a child seeing a picture of him, cast adrift in icy seas in a small open boat. He was seated at the tiller, an ageing, broken man, his long beard reaching down over his ragged clothes. His young son, equally poorly clad, sat at his feet, holding his father's hand and looking up to the old man for comfort. Near by a sick man clutched a sheepskin to cover his frail body.

History tells us that Hudson, together with his seventeen-year-old son and seven other men, were crowded into a small open boat and left to their fate on 21 June 1611, somewhere near James Bay, by a mutinous crew who then 'hastily spread canvas and fled from the scene'.

There is an Eskimo legend that some Hudson Bay Eskimos saw two white men drift ashore in a wooden boat. 'One man was dead – he had white skin, sharp features, heavy eyebrows and was heavily bearded; the other was a teenaged boy. So different were the strangers from anybody the Eskimos had ever seen that they were frightened, and fearing that the boy might be an evil spirit in human form, they

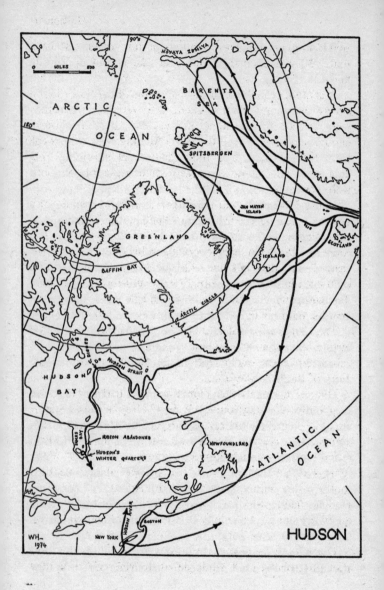

tied him up in a dog harness and kept him outside a sealskin tent.' What happened to him after that no one appears to know.

It is quite probable that the occupants of the boat did not survive very long. Four of them were very sick when they were cast adrift, and none of them was dressed in warm enough clothing to face the cold. Already they were weak from lack of food, and their chances of surviving long enough to hunt some game with their miserable weapons were very slim.

Henry Hudson began his career in 1607 as captain of a vessel owned by the Muscovy Company of London who commissioned him to sail to the far north in search of a route to China. He made two trips in his quest for a north-eastern route that took him as far as Novaya Zemlya, but on each occasion he was stopped by ice and forced to return. The company that had hired him did not wish him to repeat his failure and he had to look elsewhere for patronage.

The Dutch were quick to take on the man who had sailed farther north than any other at that time, and they gave him command of the yacht *Half Moon*, hoping to extend the glory of the Dutch Empire.

Many of the crew were Dutchmen who had served in the East Indies and they found the change from a tropical climate to a polar one too uncomfortable for their liking. On approaching Novaya Zemlya for the third time, Hudson found himself with a troublesome crew on his hands. They refused to sail farther north and he was obliged to turn south, before sailing west across the Atlantic to America. Here he made several landings, and his discoveries led to the establishment of the colony of New Amsterdam which we now know as New York.

Throughout the voyage the crew were unmanageable, and after progressing for a while down the river which is now called after him, Hudson had to return home. He arrived back on 7 November 1609.

The news of Hudson's discoveries spread quickly and everyone clamoured to hire him. Once again he found himself given command of a ship owned by a company of merchant adventurers. This time he took his son with him, sailing on the *Discovery* in search of the North-west Passage. Goodness knows why he took aboard Robert Juet as first mate – one of the troublemakers on a previous voyage. The ship sailed first to Iceland, and then on to Greenland where the ship was manoeuvred with fear and trepidation between icebergs and fields of ice.

By the time they had reached the strait which now bears Hudson's name, the crew was extremely quarrelsome and restless. First mate Juet was an active mischief-maker, accusing Hudson of favouritism. The situation worsened when the crew took fright during a storm. Nothing in their experience equalled the situation they now found themselves in. Fog blinded them, while merciless winds buffeted them towards the ice-floes. They panicked, convinced that Hudson was leading them to their deaths. He tried to encourage them with the news that they had penetrated farther into the strait than anyone had done before them, but his enthusiasm could not silence their discontent.

The discovery of Hudson Bay must have seemed to Hudson the goal they had been searching for. If it were not actually the Pacific, then it must surely soon lead to it. But his optimism was short-lived when, sailing farther into it, he reached James Bay and became trapped in the ice. Supplies of food were dwindling and although Hudson attempted to organize hunting and fishing trips, he was not too successful. Scurvy broke out amongst his frightened crew.

For months they waited and brooded, cooped up on the little ship. Every day they grew more desperate with hunger and fear. There was nothing to relieve the monotony and their thoughts turned to mutiny. Juet, the ringleader, spread the rot that blighted the men's loyalty and, with five others, he hatched a ruthless plot.

It was the middle of June before the ship could break out of the ice. Several men were sick and many were likely to die before they could return to England. To add to their troubles, they had only two weeks' provisions left. Juet knew that Hudson planned to put in at Digges Island, a bird colony they had discovered the year before, in order to re-stock with enough food for the return voyage. What bother-ed Juet was the thought that there might not be enough food to last the entire crew until they reached the island. Why, he reasoned, should the sick be allowed to shackle the strong; why should they get their share of food when they did not do their share of the work; and why sacrifice the lives of strong men for weaklings who were sure to die soon in any case? His arguments had eager listeners. They were all des-perately weighing their chances and they were prepared to go to any lengths to survive.

Inventing a story that Hudson was hoarding food for him-self and his favourites, Juet and his five conspirators per-suaded some of the others that their only chance of survival lay in casting adrift the weak and the sick as soon as the ice melted. Hudson and his son were included in the list.

On 21 June, as Hudson came out of his cabin he was seized and bound. His son, three loyal men and four sick men were bundled with him into an open boat. The only things they had with them were a light gun for shooting birds, a small amount of ammunition and meal, an iron pot, and some carpentry tools. As if ashamed of their crime, the mutineers immediately fled from the scene.

As fate would have it, they were soon to pay for their crime. Five of them, including Juet, died after being mortally wounded by natives while on Digges Island. That left only Bylot, the other conspirator and the last of the mates, in charge of the ship with only seven crew. A formidable task confronted them to get the ship back to England, but they managed this with a great deal of hardship.

On reaching port they were hauled before a court of inquiry to answer to the charge of mutiny. If justice had been done, the punishment in those days should have been hanging, but Bylot produced charts and journals of Hudson's which saved his skin. He spoke so knowledgeably about the North-west Passage, which he claimed was almost within his grasp, that his listeners were soon persuaded that he was more use alive than dead. He convinced them that he was the only man who could pilot the ship along the route where they had been with Hudson. Greed overcame the jury's indignation and Bylot's part in the mutiny was overlooked – instead he was given command of another ship.

The fate of Hudson and his poor men, however, can only be imagined. Certainly they could not have survived for long without help. Bylot promised to look for them but he never went near James Bay, and no trace was ever found of Hudson or his party. Indeed, apart from the Eskimo legend, no mention was made of them again.

The great search:
Franklin

Piece by piece, the jigsaw of the Arctic fell into shape. Whalers added some new names to the charts, but others they kept secret in order to protect themselves against competition.

During the Napoleonic wars, interest in the Arctic dropped; but it revived on the coming of peace when Britain found herself with a glut of trained seamen and with ships, and with no way of using them. The quest for a northern route to the Orient seemed the best solution to the problem, and John Franklin was asked to lead such an expedition.

So began one of the most extraordinary eras of polar exploration. Franklin's journals of the 1819–22 expedition fired the imagination of the British public with his tales of romance and tragedy. A new world was opened up – 'a wilderness of primeval beauty', where starvation turned men's minds to murder and cannibalism. So tormented were his men by hunger that they ate the remains of their old shoes, and whatever scraps of leather they had. And while Franklin marched overland to bring relief to his men, one of the Indian guides ate one of his sailors and had to be shot. The British public shrieked its indignation, and then for a while the interest in the Arctic faded.

By 1840, however, the navies of the United States and Russia posed a threat in the Arctic, and it was feared that

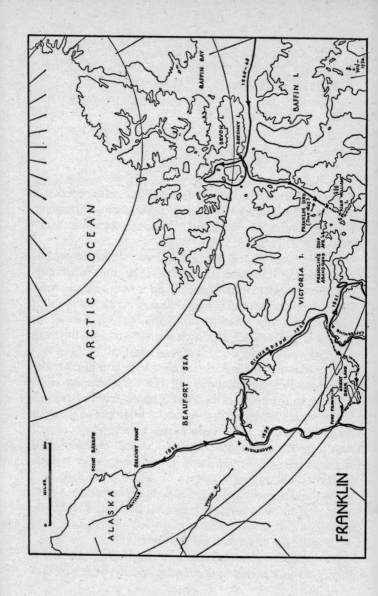

they would bag the North-west Passage for themselves. Interest again flickered. The British wanted the glory of completing the exploration of the North for themselves, and a Government-backed expedition was launched, again with Franklin in command.

By the time he had chosen to lead the British Naval Expedition of 1845, Sir John Franklin had been married several years to Jane, the daughter of a silk merchant; a girl brought up to a life of comfort, who had nevertheless travelled widely with him and had accompanied him during his posting as Governor of Tasmania – a penal settlement which lacked many of the comforts they enjoyed at home. While they were in Tasmania, they were visited by the captains of the vessels *Erebus* and *Terror* which were bound for the Antarctic to determine the position of the South Magnetic Pole. Little did Jane realize that the names of *Erebus* and *Terror* were to bring her so much anguish in the years to follow.

In 1844, soon after the Franklins returned to England, the Admiralty – urged by the Royal Geographical Society – made plans to complete the unfinished explorations of the North American Arctic coasts, with the search for the missing links to the North-west Passage as the main objective.

Magazines and newspapers launched into exciting stories about the Arctic. The ships *Erebus* and *Terror*, now returned from the Antarctic, were ordered into service with Franklin as commander. They had been modernized with steam-driven screw propellers and their cabins were warmed 'with an elaborate system of hotwater pipes'. Memories of earlier disasters made Franklin provision them for three years.

What a tragedy might have been averted had more attention been given to the necessities of the expedition, rather than to the fripperies! The vessels were as comfortably fitted out as tradition allowed; the officers' wardrooms sparkled with cut glass, china and heavy silver. The library was well stocked and each ship even had a barrel organ to entertain the men with its variety of tunes. But what was lacking were the absolute essentials: polar clothing, sledges, snowshoes and tents. And as if this were not bad enough, much of the food they carried was found, when opened, to be putrid.

Before he left Franklin seemed more anxious than usual about his wife, and he wrote to several friends asking them to look after her and comfort her should the expedition be delayed. Although he was already fifty-nine years old, he and Lady Franklin were genuinely delighted that he was to be in command of a mission of such merit, but despite their enthusiasm, the last few days before he sailed were uncomfortably tense.

Jane had made a flag for her husband to take with him to the Arctic – a tradition that most explorers followed. It was almost finished, and as she added the final stitches, Franklin who was resting on the sofa, dozed off. As he slept, she leant across and with great tenderness covered him with the flag. The movement woke him and he started. 'Why, there is a flag thrown over me,' he exclaimed. 'Don't you know that they lay the Union Jack over a corpse?'

How could Jane have known how ill-omened her gesture had been? Of the actual expedition, there is little to tell that is not tragic. By 1847, two years after her husband had sailed from England, when no news had been received of the expedition from the returning Arctic whalers, Lady Franklin and her friends began to worry. The lethargy of the Admiralty in organizing any relief stirred her into a flurry of activity. She wrote pleading for help to the Tsar of Russia, the Emperor of France, the Prime Minister of Britain and the President of the United States. So moving were her appeals that relief ships were dispatched to the north; in fact so energetic was her appeal that public prayers were offered throughout the country for those seamen serving in the Arctic.

The search dragged relentlessly on, with as many as forty expeditions seeking the missing men over the next ten years. Lady Franklin worked tirelessly to raise support. The British Government offered a reward of £20,000 for anyone who could solve the mystery of the lost expedition and bring relief to the two crews; Lady Franklin herself financed several expeditions and offered a reward of £3,000 for information that would lead to the discovery of the ships.

At last, news filtered through in 1851. On tiny Beechey Island in Barrow Strait a party from the Hudson Bay Company found gravestones carved with the names of three of Franklin's crew – near by were the remains of a camp-site. Nothing further turned up during the next three years, though the search continued over countless miles of pack ice and along hundreds of miles of Arctic coast.

In 1854 the war in Crimea diverted all the British resources, and the Government felt it could not support any further searches. However, the public responded with great sympathy to the courageous little woman whom all had come to know so well; a ballad was written and appeared for sale on the streets of London. It was called 'Lady Franklin's Lament'.

In Baffin's Bay where the whale-fish blows,
Is the fate of Franklin – no one knows.
Ten thousand pounds would I freely give,
To learn that my husband still did live.

And to bring him back to a land of life,
Where once again I would be his wife ...
I would give all the wealth I e'er shall have,
But I think, alas, he has found a grave.

Although for a while the sea search had stopped, the Hudson's Bay Company continued the search overland. People went to tremendous lengths, not only to look for the missing men, but to leave food caches for their relief. Trappers trapped foxes only to tie a collar round their necks with a note attached explaining where food had been left for the missing party. The foxes were then released in the hope that one of Franklin's men would catch one and read the note.

With every expedition, another part of the North-west Passage and its environs was discovered – till only a very small part remained uncharted.

Gradually more relics were found, and reports were heard that the men had in the last resort turned to cannibalism. The news was received with shocked protest. Embarrassed beyond measure, the Admiralty ordered a halt to the grisly business – refusing to believe that her glorious navy could sink to such an ignoble end. The reward money was paid off and the names of Franklin and his crew removed from the Naval List.

Matters would have rested there if Lady Franklin had not determined to clear her husband's name of failure. With one last desperate effort, she sank all her money into equipping the *Fox*, in the command of Captain McClintock, for a final search.

His ship got into difficulties and was beset in the ice in Bellot Strait; but he made long sledge journeys inland looking for traces of the lost expedition. He was luckier than most, and found a stone cairn containing a document which once and for all solved the mystery of Franklin's fate. It stated that Sir John Franklin died on board the *Erebus* in 1847 at the age of sixty-one. It went on to say that for nineteen months the officers and crews of the two vessels had kept to the ships which were hemmed in by ice. During that time, many of them had died of scurvy. 'They were weakened by lack of food and slowly poisoned by what they ate.' Starvation compelled the 105 survivors to abandon their ships on 22 April 1848. It was a miserable procession that started out across the ice, dragging their boats, which in places would be needed to ferry them. Ahead of them they faced a trek of 250 miles (400 kilometres) towards the mouth of the Back river, where they hoped to find assistance. They were starving and too weak to carry much weight. A grim trail of discarded clothes, stoves and tents led up to the frail corpses of the men, frozen into the tundra in the attitudes in which they fell. The Eskimos discovered them, and when McClintock arrived amongst them, they therefore had grim news to tell.

McClintock returned with relics to back up the horrifying stories he had to report. His findings, though tragic, were welcomed by Lady Franklin. They proved beyond doubt that in sacrificing their lives, Franklin and his men had forged the final link in the chain that opened up the North-west Passage.

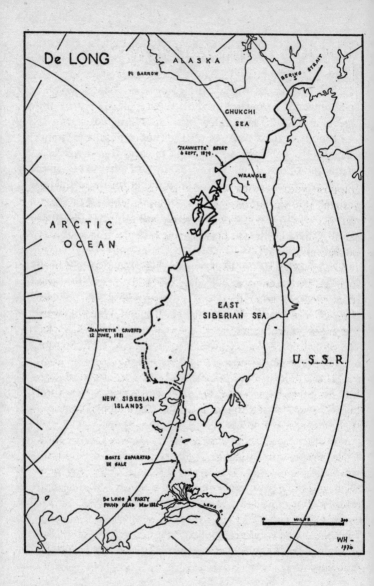

The loss of the *Jeannette:*
De Long

Suppose your mother was so anxious about you hurting yourself that she stopped you from playing with other children, discouraged you from running, swimming, boating or skating, and kept you at home as much as possible with only books as playthings.

George Washington De Long, an American explorer born in 1844, had such an upbringing. So tame and solitary was his existence at home that his only brush with adventure was through the stories he devoured. His only friends were imaginary ones, summoned from the pages of his books. Not surprisingly, George De Long developed a passion for sea stories, which in turn gave him a burning desire to go to sea. It is ironic that the books which were intended to keep him happy at home were the very instruments which fired his ambition to enter the most dangerous of all professions – that of a naval explorer.

Naturally his parents were violently opposed to the idea. They forbade him to enlist during the Civil War, and only when they knew that all places at the Naval Academy were filled, did they grudgingly allow him to apply. After several refusals, but still determined not to accept defeat, he secured a personal interview with the Secretary of the Navy. The latter was so impressed with the determination of the young man that he ordered his immediate acceptance at the Academy.

George De Long graduated with distinction in 1865, and got his first taste of the Arctic in 1873, when as Lieutenant on the *Juniata*, he went to the relief of the *Polaris*, a ship lost off the coast of Greenland. Lieutenant De Long volunteered to take command of the search party which left the ship at Upernavik, halfway up the coast of West Greenland, and took a small ship's boat northwards in the direction of Melville Bay – a notoriously dangerous place known as the 'Whalers' Graveyard'.

In a letter to his wife, he described the difficulties of that boat journey – a journey which was ten days of physical torture – cooped up in a small open boat, battling through ice-filled waters. Most of the time they were wet to the skin with rain or spray – their only covering a thick blanket of fog. Sleep was almost impossible with so many hazards surrounding them, and what moments they could snatch were an agony, as they banged and bruised themselves against the lumps of wet coal which filled every nook and cranny. (The coal was needed to drive the engine to enable them to travel as far as possible.)

Fog hid the icebergs and disguised the danger as they drifted among the ice-floes; it muffled the sounds of the ice which thickened around them, squeezing them in and threatening any moment to crush them. It was a frightening struggle for the occupants of the little boat to ram their way through ice which in some places reached a thickness of 4 feet (1·2 metres). De Long knew that if he could not break free they faced the possibility of being crushed by the ice or being starved or frozen to death.

When they finally made their way out of the ice they found themselves in a heavy sea. Frantically they battled to keep the boat afloat in waves which almost swamped her. Half the crew baled while the rest struggled with sails and oars to keep her from smashing into the sides of the icebergs which surrounded them. So strong was the wind that it dashed the waves over the tops of the hundred-foot bergs.

Ahead of them lay the pack-ice, and as the current drew them closer to its edge, they were mesmerized by the frightening spectacle. Huge pieces of ice were constantly broken off by the waves and dashed against the pack, only to be ground to powder.

The storm lasted thirty hours and left the men perishingly cold and exhausted. When the wind broke, De Long gave orders to return to the ship. A less competent man could not have tackled such a perilous situation and survived; but De Long combined the knowledge of good seamanship with the judgement and courage of a good leader.

These same qualities distinguished his tragic expedition to the Arctic a few years later, in 1879, when he endeavoured to reach the North Pole.

At the time De Long sailed on this expedition, there was still very little known about the Arctic Ocean, its size or character. The most popular view was that a belt of loose ice surrounded a huge continental land mass which stretched for some 2,000 miles (3,200 kilometres) across the Arctic and was joined on to Greenland. Somewhere on that land mass lay the North Pole.

De Long planned to sail through the relatively unknown Bering Strait until he reached Wrangel Land (really an island), which he believed to be the tip of this great land mass. From here he would sledge first to the Pole and then on to Greenland.

Little did he know that he was sailing into an area of 5,500,000 square miles (14,000,000 square kilometres) of heaving sea ice and that the North Pole was not on land at all. In 1879 De Long's ship the *Jeannette* was beset in the ice at longitude 71°35′ N, and latitude 175°5′ W.

For the whole of their long imprisonment De Long encouraged his men to carry out the scientific work they had set themselves. Even so, the months dragged by monotonously. All around them they could hear the sounds of ice being squeezed together as if by giant hands. Great masses of it would suddenly rise in the air, forced upwards into walls of jostling, tumbling debris. This activity would be accompanied by terrifying noises as the ice rumbled, shrieked and groaned.

It was especially frightening in winter because for five months at that latitude the sun does not rise in the Arctic. They lived in terror of pressure ridges ploughing through the ice towards them or of 'masses of ice building up to tower over them and topple upon them'. At times the ship 'shook and trembled like a reed'.

After twenty-one months of captivity, the ship was crushed. The officers and crew calmly abandoned it, dividing up into three parties, each with boat and sledges. For three months they dragged their heavy boats and loads over broken and shifting fields of ice, suffering hardship and hunger. They had set their course for the New Siberian Islands but often they were carried out of their way by the drifting pack. Storms, fogs and snow plagued them, hindering their progress and making them weak from hunger, cold and fatigue. But throughout all this De Long kept the men's spirits from flagging and encouraged them by his own fine example.

Despite the dreadful physical hardships, the preservation of the scientific data they had so painstakingly recorded was put above their own comfort. And although the men's limbs ached and every step was an agony for frostbitten feet, they carried the valuable records safely to land, on the Siberian coast. Tragically two-thirds of the ship's company, among them De Long, died from hunger and exposure on reaching land, within a day's march of safety. By a cruel stroke of fate, the map of the region which they possessed did not show the nearest village, or they might have survived. As it was, De Long's days were spent comforting his dying men until he, too, was forced to give up the struggle.

Ironically, the very current which destroyed the ship off the Siberian islands also carried the wreckage across the Arctic Ocean to Greenland, and so completed, after De Long's death, the journey which he had set his heart on.

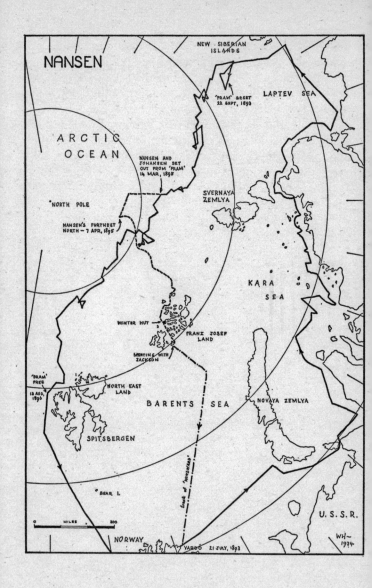

A strange encounter: Nansen

Imagine your alarm and disbelief if, hundreds of miles away from civilization, on an unexplored island covered with snow and ice and surrounded by freezing seas, there emerged from behind a hummock a man – a wild man, who staggered towards you in dirty, foul-smelling rags, his long hair caked with fat and his face hidden by layers of soot.

Such a sight met Frederick Jackson, leader of the British Expedition to Franz Josef Land, when he was out exploring with his sledge dogs, on 17 June 1895. His shock was all the greater when the stranger spoke – addressing him, by name, in perfect English.

It did not take the Englishman long to recognize, behind the unkempt appearance of the strange man, one of the most famous explorers of the day – Fridtjof Nansen, a young Norwegian. Jackson had met Nansen in England after the Norwegian had become the first to cross the Greenland Icecap a few years before.

For Nansen, this chance encounter was the climax of his greatest adventure – an adventure for which he had been preparing since his days as a schoolboy when he used to go off into the hills of his native Norway to ski and be alone, and to dream of being an explorer.

The dream became reality in June 1893 when Nansen, on board the *Fram*, sailed north from Norway to cross the unexplored Arctic Ocean. No one had yet discovered what lay around the North Pole, though many had died in attempting to find out. The memory of De Long and the ill-fated *Jeannette* was enough to frighten most people, but for Nansen it provided a clue to the riddle of the North, a riddle he was determined to solve.

Three years after the sinking of the *Jeannette*, pieces of its wreckage were found embedded in ice-floes off the west coast of Greenland. Nansen believed they had drifted across the Arctic Ocean, via the Pole, to Spitzbergen, and from there down the east coast of Greenland, round the tip of the island and up along the west coast.

He announced he would take a specially designed vessel that would be able to withstand the pressure of being frozen into the Arctic pack, and he would try to drift across the Pole from east to west, thus establishing that the current ran in this direction over the Pole, and that the area was covered with sea, not land.

The world received his challenge with excitement. Nansen combed shipyards for a shipbuilder who could create the impossible, for a man who could build a ship so strong that no pressure could crush her, 'with a hull so smooth that it could slip like an eel out of the embrace of ice'. He found the man – and the *Fram* was such a ship.

On 24 June 1893, the *Fram* turned north from Norway and made her way towards the Kara Sea – on and on through seas no ship had sailed before. The ship stood up to the ice well, 'twisting and turning like a ball on a platter', till she was allowed to become frozen in – just 100 miles (160 kilometres) short of the New Siberian Islands. The ice thickened around the *Fram*, imprisoning her in its grip – the same ice that had crushed the *Jeannette* and forced many of her gallant crew to march across its milling surface to their deaths.

But, unlike previous ships that had tried to avoid the ice,

the *Fram* gave herself up to its clutches, confident that in her leader, Fridtjof Nansen, she had a man whose judgement she could trust. It was an enormous gamble those thirteen brave men took. If they were successful they would have broken through the veil of the unknown and brought back Knowledge, its greatest treasure, but if they failed – who could tell what would be their fate?

Throughout the long, dark winter the ship became a hive of activity as each man threw himself into some branch of scientific investigation. Food was good, the ship was comfortable, and they carried supplies for five years. A newspaper was printed, polar bears were hunted, and birthdays and saints' days celebrated. Every day new data was stored in the scientific bank.

The crew became accustomed to the terrifying groans and rumbles of the ice as it was squeezed up into mountainous ridges, creating a cacophony of sound which disturbed the otherwise deathly silence. Several times huge masses of ice roared out of the darkness towards the helpless ship, towering over her and threatening all the crew with imminent death. Nansen describes the terror: 'You jump back to save yourself. But the ice splits in front of you, a black gulf opens, and up streams water. You turn in another direction, and there through the darkness you can just make out a new ridge moving towards you. You turn in another direction, and there is the ridge again ...'

For months the *Fram* drifted, sometimes forwards in the direction they wanted, and at other times back the way they had come. Nansen, an active person, suffered the monotony of their forward drift and fretted when they moved backwards. But as the weeks passed, the drift to the north and west drew them inexorably towards the heart of the ocean.

Nansen began to establish the true nature of the Arctic Ocean – a deep sea, free of islands and bisected by a strong current. Although they hoped to reach the Pole, it was not the absolute object of the expedition. As time wore on and it became apparent that the ship would drift past the Pole, and not over it, Nansen's pulse quickened with a new ambition.

For a long while life had been routine on the ship and Nansen was becoming bored. By the end of a year, he had proved his theory of the polar current to be right, and by that time too the *Fram* had proved her ability to survive the ice. There seemed nothing more but to live out the passing of the days till they arrived safely home. Nansen could not be satisfied with that, however. Instead he burned with an unrest which made him almost despair. He felt as if his life had stopped and as if the ship had become a tomb. Not even the beauty of the Arctic night could calm his taut nerves – beauty that had made him remark, 'The Arctic night is like a dream . . . with a peace that passes all understanding.'

This peace, however, was not enough to keep Nansen on the ship; restless for change and excitement, he decided to make a dash for the Pole.

Leaving his ship in the charge of Sverdrup, a highly experienced and competent captain, Nansen set out across the ice with one companion on 14 March 1895 in the direction of the Pole. The trip would be risky. Once they left the ship there would be no way for them to find their way back to it over the drifting ice. They would be completely on their own, except for twenty-eight dogs with whom they would have to make their return across the ice to Franz Josef Land or Novaya Zemlya – a round trip of over 1,000 miles (1,600 kilometres).

Taking three sledges and two kayaks, one tent, and provisions for one hundred days, Nansen and Johansen set off. 'It is like bidding farewell to a dear friend and to a home,' he commented on leaving the *Fram*, the ship which had brought him farther north than any other man had been before.

It was now that Nansen's childhood experience of skiing and living the outdoor life was to stand him in good stead, as he and his companion set off with dog-sledge and skis. Their route wove across constantly shifting ice where there would be nobody to come to their help if they should get into difficulties.

At first the going was good, but it was not long before their way was blocked by pressure ridges, hummocks and loose ice. The cold transformed their clothes into an armour of ice during the day, which melted into wet bandages at night in their tents. Their sleeping bags grew heavier and heavier from the moisture of their breath, which collected on the inside of the bags and froze.

As dogs began to weaken they were killed and fed to the others – there was a limited amount of dog food and only by feeding dog to dog could they extend their march. The going was miserable and they several times crashed through cracks and pitfalls, on escaping from which their legs became encased in a mass of ice. As hard as they struggled forward, they found the drift carried them back, until on 8 April, 226 miles (363 kilometres) from the North Pole, they called a halt.

They had already killed several of their dogs and had travelled 200 miles (320 kilometres) farther north than any man before them, but this was the end of the road. Beyond lay an impenetrable jumble of ice which continued as far as the eye could see.

After a ceremonial feast, Nansen moved southwards, hoping to cover the 415 miles to Franz Josef Land in about ninety days. He made steady progress for a while, stopping from time to time to calculate his position and to plot his route. A serious problem arose when they forgot to wind their chronometers: this was to complicate their navigation; but an even worse disaster fell when they discovered that they had left their compass on the ice. It was a very anxious period until Nansen found it, having had to retrace his route for two days. But by good luck it had not sunk through the ice, or been carried off-route.

Strong though both men were, it was tough dragging and pushing the sledges over the ridges and floundering through the fields of loose ice. Meanwhile, their food was diminishing and with it the number of dogs. They were seriously worried that they might not reach Franz Josef Land, as the drift showed signs of carrying them past the island before they would have a chance to scramble ashore.

As it was difficult to manoeuvre three sledges, they decided to abandon one, but not before they had made a fire with it to warm their frozen limbs. In the dramatic fire they not only burnt the tent, but they nearly fell through the hole in the ice caused by the heat.

By the end of May they had begun to meet huge stretches of water. The time had come to mend the kayaks which had been badly holed on the rough ice when the sledges, with the kayaks on top, had capsized earlier in the journey. When they did take to the water, after discarding as much as they could of their loads, the kayaks were lashed together side by side, with the sledges across them, and the three remaining dogs inside.

The frail vessels soon began to leak, but the men paddled on, keeping them afloat by constantly baling. Food was low, so when Nansen shot a seal that surfaced nearby, they dined royally, forgetting the hazards of the voyage as they sat in their tent on the ice eating blood pancakes with sugar.

For the next few weeks they struggled through rain and mist – at times through slush, at other times through grinding ice. Walrus frequently attacked the kayaks, nearly sinking them and on one occasion Johansen was very nearly killed by a polar bear. But they slogged on, sighting land on 6 August. By the end of the month they were still 150 miles (240 kilometres) short of Franz Josef Land, their goal. However, forced ashore by bad weather they knew not where, they decided to dig themselves in for the winter.

They dug a rectangular hole in the ground around which they piled up stones, making a stone igloo in which to live. For nine months they survived the misery of this hovel, melting walrus blubber for lighting and heat. Walrus and polar bear provided their main source of food and fuel and the men made the hut more habitable by filling in the crevices between the stones with moss and earth, and by covering the roof with a stretched walrus skin. Soon their clothes became saturated in fat, oil and blood. Occasionally they went for walks, but the wind tore through their tattered clothing, making an agony out of the exercise. On many days their only excursions were to collect ice for water or meat and blubber for food and fuel.

As winter, with its near-endless dark, set in, their thoughts turned frequently to the *Fram* and the mates they had left with her. How different their situations were now! Here there was so little to interest them as month dragged into month, except the marauding foxes and the inquisitive polar bears. For a Christmas celebration they scraped the grease off their shirts and turned them inside out, washing themselves in a cupful of hot water. No matter what they did, they could not get rid of the layers of fat and soot that clung to them. They slept long hours and never quarrelled.

As spring daylight began to return, their thoughts turned to travel, but it was not until 19 May, that, clad in a strange assortment of fur clothes made during the winter, Nansen and Johansen finally set off again. They left a brief note of their experiences and plans in the hut, in case other explorers should stumble upon their stone igloo here.

Their goal was Spitzbergen. After travelling 70 or 80 miles (about 120 kilometres) they came to open water and took to the kayaks. Disaster nearly overtook them during one of their pauses to reconnoitre. They climbed onto an ice-floe to look around, and the kayaks drifted away out of reach and were caught in a strong current. Nansen dived into the icy water after them, for to lose the kayaks would mean certain death. With each stroke his limbs grew weaker, until it looked as if Johansen would lose not only his sole means of escape but also his good friend. As Nansen frantically struck out, his arms and legs gradually grew numb and began to stiffen. He gasped for breath, knowing that at any moment the struggle would be over – two minutes in that icy water would have killed most people. The kayaks were still out of reach and Nansen had to turn on his back to keep from sinking with exhaustion. Out of the corner of his eye he could see his friend frantically pacing the floe. The vision seemed to encourage him and, turning to swim again, he redoubled his efforts. Nansen says: 'The strokes became more and more feeble, but the distance became shorter and shorter'. At last he was able to stretch out an arm and grasp the boat. He pulled himself up and lay there a few seconds before he had the strength to clamber in. After a few minutes, he paddled back to his companion.

The dangers were not over, however, because a few days later a walrus struck Nansen's kayak a savage blow, holing it. As the water trickled in Nansen managed to scramble out onto a nearby floe. As he did so the kayak sank. Luck must have been on his side, because the craft lodged on a sunken ridge and was easy to recover. The gash was soon repaired, but the two men were anxious to have no more mishaps before they reached land! The next day, 17 June, Nansen recalls they 'encamped in a land which I believed to be unseen by human eye and untrodden by human foot, when a sound reached my ears like the barking of a dog. I strained my ears but heard no more. I thought I must have been mistaken ... but then the barking came again, and there was no longer room for doubt.'

Scrambling over the icy hummocks in pursuit of the sound, it was then that Nansen came face to face with Frederick Jackson. And a very lucky meeting it was, too, because as Jackson said, 'Had he missed us, it is doubtful if he could ever have left Franz Josef Land; for some 160 miles (250 kilometres) of open sea lies between these islands and the nearest known land: a sea which cannot be crossed in leaky canvas canoes.'

A few weeks later, Nansen and Johansen sailed for home on the relief ship, *Windward*, which had arrived to take back Jackson's party.

After a voyage of nearly three years they were back in Norway. Nansen's happiness was matched by his anxiety for news of the *Fram*. It came a week later in the form of a telegram:

FRAM ARRIVED IN GOOD CONDITION. ALL WELL ON BOARD. SHALL START AT ONCE FOR TROMSØ. WELCOME HOME. OTTO SVERDRUP.

The ship and all her passengers were safe. After drifting for practically three years, the *Fram* had at last broken free of the ice near the north coast of Spitzbergen. One of the greatest sagas of exploration was complete.

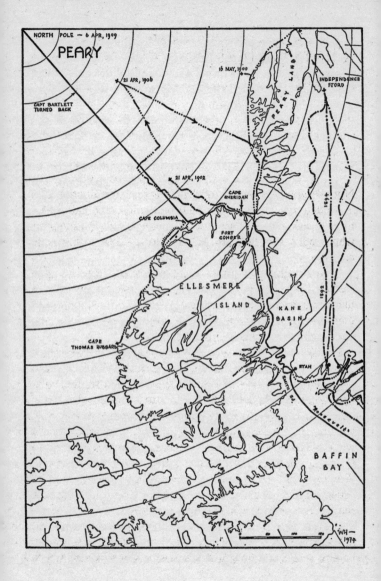

The tarnished prize:
Peary

Not everybody is capable of the effort or determination that is needed to pursue an ambition that could take half a lifetime to achieve; but Robert Edwin Peary was a man for whom fame was not just an idle dream, but a desperate craving.

'I would like to acquire a name which would be an open sesame to circles of culture and refinement anywhere, a name which would make my mother proud and which would make me feel that I was the peer of anyone I might meet,' he wrote when he was a young man.

He did fulfil this desire, but not without great sacrifice both to himself and to his family. Born in Pennsylvania in 1856, Peary was brought up by his widowed mother who doted on him. Maybe it was her treatment of him that made him rebellious – she reared him as if he were a little girl, teaching him sewing and insisting that he wore a bonnet when playing in the sun, to protect his fair skin. To add to Peary's embarrassment, he had a lisp which he did everything possible to overcome, but still his school fellows called him a 'cissy', and it was only by becoming a fighter that he managed to silence their insults.

By the time he left school his thoughts had turned to adventure, and he joined the Navy as a civil engineer to begin a career of unimaginable hardship. Peary's early hopes of finding fame by becoming the first to cross the Greenland Icecap were dashed by the news that Nansen had forestalled him. However, there was still much exploration to be done in Greenland and Peary devoted years to unravelling the mysteries of the north of Greenland, earning for himself a reputation as a tough and fearless explorer.

Peary made his second expedition to Greenland in 1891. Before going ashore, an accident on board ship trapped Peary's leg against the wheelhouse; the bones had to be snapped before he could be extricated. The leg was put in splints, Peary was strapped to a board which was lowered into a boat, and he was then rowed ashore. Frederick Cook, the expedition doctor, cared for him and soon got him fit enough to travel into the icy interior of the country. Neither man knew then that they would become rivals for the most cherished prize of any explorer – the discovery of the North Pole.

Peary's wife Jo accompanied him on this expedition and she had her first baby among the Eskimos. Peary spent many years living and travelling with the Eskimos, learning from them techniques of dog driving as well as how to survive in one of the most inhospitable regions in the world. In a tremendous journey across the icecap, he discovered the northern coast of Greenland and proved, once and for all, that Greenland was an island and that it did not stretch, as some believed, all the way to the North Pole.

The explorer was showered with honours for his pioneering work, but he still felt the need to do something 'big' that would make him famous for all time; and with that in mind, he diverted his energies towards an assault on the North Pole.

He planned to sail as far north as he could through Baffin Bay, Smith Sound and Kane Basin, ramming his ship through the ice towards the northern tip of Greenland or

Ellesmere Island, where he could establish a base. If he were unsuccessful one year, he would try again the next, and keep trying until his ambition was achieved.

In 1898 he sailed north in the *Windward* but was stopped by ice from entering Kennedy Channel, and he had to winter at Cape D'Urville, far short of his destination. Peary hated the forced inactivity, but could not travel north by sledge to set up an advance base until the ice was good. He planned to sledge 250 miles (400 kilometres) to Fort Conger on Ellesmere Island, where an American expedition led by Greely fifteen years earlier had established a base – an expedition where most of the men had died of starvation on leaving camp, while many of the living, in order to survive, had resorted to cannibalism.

It was midwinter before Peary and his expedition could set out on the journey north. There was no sun to warm their freezing bodies or to light their way, and so they had to travel in moonlight. For nine days they struggled over appalling ice; rations were low – they were still only half way – and there remained only two more days of moonlight. The wind cut through their clothes, chilling them to the bone and blinding them with drift. They staggered on, growing more and more exhausted. For eight more days they toiled in the dark through a chaos of churned-up sea-ice, collapsing almost under the strain of dragging the sledges across the rubble of ice: two dogs died in their tracks and the others were too weak to pull. The camps on the ice were so cold that the men could not sleep. But just when all hope seemed lost, on 6 January 1899, they stumbled into the hut they had been seeking.

The relief they felt on arriving at their destination was sobered by the reminders of the grim fate of the previous men who had lived there. The floor was littered with food boxes and cast-off clothing, and from the scattered confusion of the gear it was evident that the men had made a hasty departure. But at least for Peary's party there was food and shelter.

It was only when their bodies were beginning to thaw that Peary noticed a strange wooden feeling in his legs – it proved to be frostbite. The doctor removed the frost and bathed the feet but there was no way of saving the toes – most would have to be amputated. The operation was crudely performed with what tools were available and for six weeks Peary lay on his back in great pain wondering how he would ever walk again. For six weeks they were 'snow-bound, stormbound and nightbound' – and all the time Peary pondered about his future. Even in his crippled condition, his thoughts turned to his ambition, and defiantly he scrawled in Latin on the wall: 'I shall find a way or make one'.

The return to the ship was agonizing. Peary was lashed to a sledge and tended across the awful ice by his men. In spite of their care, they slammed into ice ridges and knocked against other barriers; every jolt was torture to Peary's tender stumps, though he did not complain even when the sledge overbalanced and dragged him along with it down to the bottom of a snow slope.

It took eleven days to return to the ship where Peary had a more sophisticated operation on his toes. 'All but the little toe on each foot was removed.' A month later, he was up and about even before the stumps could heal. He made several journeys riding on the sledges, and when he walked he used crutches.

For the whole of the summer he made long exploratory journeys, mapping stretches of the North Greenland coast and getting his first taste of travelling on the ice of the Arctic Ocean. His feet were bruised with walking, and occasional blows against the ice struck his amputated toes and made him 'sick to his stomach and half blind with pain'.

From the northernmost point of Greenland, Peary looked out over the jostling mass of broken-up ice that separated him from the Pole. He felt sure he could get there, if he could use a team of supporting parties to assist him in relaying the vital loads to a point far out on the ice, from which he could make a dash for the Pole. While he delayed in the north he heard of the death of his second child. He was heartbroken. The sudden death of his mother only added to his grief and he returned home.

If Jo Peary and her daughter hoped he had returned for good, they were soon to be disappointed. Over the years, Peary had found some staunch supporters amongst influential men and even President Roosevelt had become excited by the possibility of an American victory at the North Pole. Jo begged her husband not to let life slip by them, and even his daughter pleaded that she needed him. But Peary's mind was made up. 'I am as strong as ever in my belief that the Pole can be secured by a determined effort via the Smith Sound gateway and that it ought to be done and must be secured for this country,' he argued. And in his orders from the Navy, of which he had been an absentee member for so many years, he was directed: 'The attainment of the Pole should be your main object. Nothing short will suffice . . . our national pride is involved in the undertaking.' It was with this enormous burden of emotion that Peary once again turned north.

He planned his attack on the Pole as a general might attack a remote, impregnable fortress. Transport, food and equipment were the three vital factors where he needed all his knowledge and experience to make the right decisions. The ship, named the *Roosevelt* after the President, was specially modified to enable her to ram her way through the ice and survive the pressure of the pack. Peary had worked

out a system of travelling with relaying support parties
which would leave him free to make the last final 'dash' for
the Pole. Everything seemed set for a brilliant climax to the
long struggle.

The ship sailed from New York on 16 July 1905 and re-
acted to the ice as Peary had hoped, squeezing and twisting
her way northward. There were some anxious moments
before the ship settled into winter quarters, when it was
nipped by the ice, forced upwards and 'left vibrating like a
violin', but no damage was done. At the start of the winter,
there were two hundred Eskimo dogs and over a hundred
Eskimos, including women and children, on board. All
would play their part in the general plan of hunting and
making clothes and caring for Peary ashore, until the able-
bodied men amongst them could act as porters on his trip
to the Pole.

The winter passed with great games and festivities to
keep everyone amused and then, on 19 February 1906, the
first of the support parties left the ship to set up stations 50
miles (80 kilometres) apart along a direct route to the Pole.
The idea was good in theory but impracticable, because
Peary had reckoned without the easterly drift of the pack-
ice, which made it impossible to keep a route open to the
north. For days the various parties were stopped by blizzards
but still Peary clung to his idea of making a dash for the
Pole. The effort was too much, however, and he had to turn
back, short of food, obliged to eat some of the dogs and to
break some of the sledges to burn as fuel.

Lack of provisions prevented his waiting in the Arctic
another year in order to make another attempt – he decided
to go back and raise more money to equip a final expedition.
By now he was desperate. He was growing old and there
would not be more than one more chance to win his prize.
As he made his plans he talked of the discovery of the Pole

as 'the thing which it is intended that I should do, and the thing that I must do.' Jo was marvellously encouraging, although she felt he was a great enough explorer already.

In America eager admirers were willing to accept that he had the Pole within his reach now that he had replanned his campaign; and to show their encouragement, the President and his family came aboard to say goodbye. Only one thing disturbed Peary's repose, and that was the sudden emergence of a rival.

For many years Peary had been blazing a trail in North-west Greenland and along the coast of Ellesmere Island, which he decided would be the route he would follow to the Pole. This trail, he felt, belonged to him. You can imagine his anger, therefore, when he heard that Dr Frederick Cook, his earlier companion, had left on a trip to the Arctic with the intention of trying for the Pole.

Many of Peary's supporters already recognized Cook as a serious threat and they began a campaign to discredit him as a liar. Peary at first could not believe there was any truth in the rumour that he had a rival and when he did at last acknowledge the competition he was exceedingly indignant. Not only was Cook trespassing in an area Peary regarded as his own domain, but he was using dogs and Eskimos that Peary could otherwise have used. In panic, it seemed, he wrote a note to the President warning him against Cook and sent this back with his supporting ship.

Cook had set off for the Pole several months before Peary reached Greenland and there was nothing Peary could do but get on with his own plans. This time he decided he would leave from Cape Columbia, a distance of 413 nautical miles (760 kilometres) from the Pole. He would again use supporting parties but, unlike the previous attempt, they would stay closer together, so as not to be separated when the ice cracked open. Bartlett, an Englishman – the captain of the *Roosevelt* – was to pioneer 10 miles (16 kilometres) of the route each day until the main party caught up with him. This meant chopping a way through enormous walls of ice so that those that followed would not be delayed. Even with this method, those behind sometimes had to blaze a new trail, because the drifting ice had altered the area between them and Bartlett. Peary was to save himself for the final dash to the Pole which he had decided to make with Matthew Henson, his Negro manservant, and four Eskimos. He felt very strongly that the achievement should be an American one, and it was probably with this in mind that on 1 April, at latitude 87° 46' 49" N, Peary asked Bartlett to return to Base.

It seemed a harsh decision for Bartlett to be turned back now when he had pioneered the whole of the route to a distance of 153 statute miles (245 kilometres) from the Pole. Certainly Bartlett had kept up a good pace and Peary admitted that he was 'obliged repeatedly to jump on the sledges to keep up.' Peary's feet had long healed, of course, but it was difficult for him to move quickly. However, Peary argued later, when confronted by critics, that to have taken on Bartlett and his two Eskimos would have put all their lives in jeopardy, as they would not have had enough food for all to return safely to land.

Imagine yourself in Peary's position after Bartlett left. You are standing on the edge of a circle which, from your navigator's last calculation, you know has a radius of 153 statute miles. At the centre of that circle is the North Pole. But since that circle on which you are standing is only an imaginary line, how are you to know in which direction to go to arrive exactly at the North Pole? The only sure way is to calculate your longitude from the height of the sun at a precise moment of Greenwich Mean Time, for with both your latitude and your longitude known, it is easy enough to calculate which way to go to reach the North Pole.

But this Peary did not do. He simply assumed that he was still on the longitude of Cape Columbia where he had set off, and assumed he was heading for the Pole. If, however, the detours he had made as he wove through the broken pack-ice had zigged more than they had zagged, and the drift of the ice had carried him still further off his straight-line course from Cape Columbia to the Pole – then he would throughout his journey have been heading in the wrong direction and would never have hit the North Pole.

And is this what happened? We do not know. Peary claims that he reached the North Pole on 6 April 1909 and his claim cannot be disproved – even though the distances he says he travelled to reach the Pole by that date are truly phenomenal. Over a period of four successive days from 6 to 9 April, he claims to have averaged over fifty-seven statute miles a day without any allowance for detours around obstacles that lay in his way. Even his daily average over the whole distance on the polar pack has never been equalled in a single day's march by anyone before or since. The trouble was, it was not witnessed.

But if this last great effort had pushed him to the very limit of his endurance, a far greater test of character was still awaiting him, for five days before he announced to the world that he had reached the Pole, Dr Frederick Cook had announced that he, with only two Eskimos, had reached it the year before.

Peary's amazement at finding that Cook was believed and he was not sent him almost mad with rage. In a public statement he announced Cook was a liar. A furious battle started with supporters on either side leaping to the defence of their hero. As it happened, Peary's followers were the most influential. They organized a vicious campaign against Cook which people believed. Peary's claim was officially accepted and the man heaped with honours. But victory was not sweet, however, and as the years passed the victorious explorer rarely spoke of the prize that had lost its glitter.

The unsung hero: Cook

Many people can look back on their lives and point out an event which dramatically changed their careers. Dr Frederick Cook, the American explorer, had many reasons to remember the effect his first meeting with Peary was to have on his life.

As a child, Cook had not been happy; he came from a poor family and his early years were marred by the constant need to scrimp and save to keep alive. The death of his father when he was young put the burden of earning a living heavily on his shoulders and he sold fruit at a market until he could enter the dairy business in Brooklyn. With the money he saved he managed to support himself while he studied medicine, but even when he had qualified as a doctor he could barely earn enough to make ends meet.

There seemed no possible solution to his problem, till one day he read that Robert Peary was preparing an expedition to the Arctic. The year was 1891 and Cook was twenty-six. All the dormant ambition he had had as a boy to be an explorer welled up in him and he volunteered as Expedition Surgeon. On his acceptance for the job, Cook described feeling 'as though a door to a prison cell had been opened'. No sense of foreboding warned him that the path he was to follow would lead several years later to a real prison cell.

The expedition took Cook to Greenland, where he was

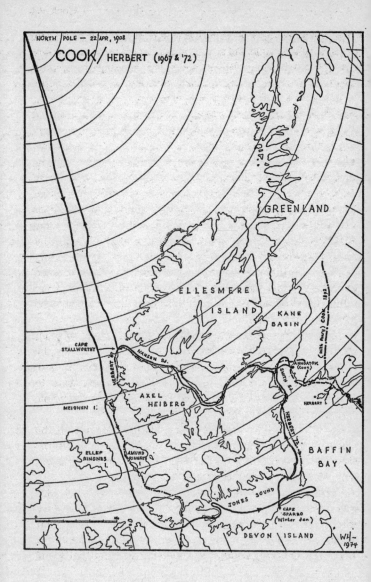

NORTH POLE — 22 APR. 1908

COOK/HERBERT (1967 & '72)

GREENLAND

ELLESMERE ISLAND

KANE BASIN

CAPE STALLWORTHY

NANSEN Sd.

HERBERT '67

ANNOATOK (Cook)

SMITH Sd.

(with Peary) COOK 1892

AXEL HEIBERG

MEIGHEN I.

HERBERT I.

HERBERT '72

BAFFIN BAY

ELLEF RINGNES I.

AMUND RINGNES I.

JONES SOUND

CAPE SPARBO (Winter Den)

DEVON ISLAND

WH— 1974

soon given a chance to show his worth. When Peary severely mangled his leg in an accident on board ship just before going ashore, Cook carefully set the broken bones and, with tremendous care, saved Peary from being crippled for life.

Peary could not help being impressed by the young doctor who was a hard worker and always helpful; and he admired Cook's 'unruffled patience and coolness in an emergency'. Cook, on his part, soon succumbed to the spell of the Arctic and, fevered with the excitement of exploring new land, he decided he would devote his career to exploration. From 1893 till 1906 his life was taken up with various expeditions: two trips to Greenland, organized by himself; two years as surgeon on the Belgian Antarctic Expedition where he met Roald Amundsen, the great Norwegian explorer; another trip to Greenland with Peary; two attempts at Mount McKinley – the highest mountain in Alaska – which he climbed successfully in 1906. Many were to question this achievement but evidence brought to light over the years showed his claim to be true.

Throughout all these expeditions Cook served without pay, and although his fortune remained as scant as ever, he felt the work itself was reward enough. His wants were simple and his ambition easily satisfied. Events were to happen before long, however, which would alter the whole circumstances of his life.

By the time Peary was planning his final assault on the Pole, Dr Frederick Cook had sailed for Annoatok in Northwest Greenland with John R. Bradley, a wealthy sportsman who wanted to go north to hunt big game.

Halfway up the west coast of Greenland, Cook described his feelings as he gazed at the awesome beauty around him: 'For hours I stood on deck alone. The golden colours of the midnight sun suffused my mind, and I swam in a sea of molten glitter. I was consumed for hours by but one yearning – a yearning that filled and intoxicated me – to go on, and on, and ever onward, where no man had ever been.' From then onwards he knew he must try to reach the Pole.

At Annoatok the idea became more firmly impressed on his mind as he gazed at the most northerly Eskimo settlement in the world. Here was meat in plenty, 'strewn along the shore under mounds of stone'; here were hunters strong enough to be good helpers with the best dog teams he had seen along the coast. This would be the ideal base to start from; there was unlimited food and plenty of furs for clothing.

When the ship turned back, Cook was left behind with one companion, a young German named Rudolph Francke. There was no time to be homesick as they worked to build a hut and to get a base established. Cook would need men and dogs on his trip to the Pole and he wanted to make sure that they all started off in superb condition, fed on lashings of fresh meat beforehand to build up their strength.

Throughout the autumn and winter, huge stacks of walrus, seal, narwhal and white whale were cached for the great journey. While the men hunted, the women gathered grass to pad boots and mittens, collected moss wicks for the Eskimo lamps and sewed endless fur clothes for the ordeal ahead. Sleeping bags were made from reindeer skin and sewn with sinew. The whole village was involved in the preparations and as Cook saw how well things were progressing he felt an exhilaration that he had never known before.

As winter set in and the Eskimos changed from living in their summer tents to their winter igloos made of stone and moss, Cook learnt how to adapt himself. He ate frozen meat like them, dressed in shirts made of soft birdskins, trousers made of bearskin, boots of sealskin and stockings of hareskin. When travelling, he wore a parka made either of reindeer or fox fur.

He accompanied the Eskimos on bear hunts, building up his stamina on forced marches; and when the desperate chase started as the dogs scented the bear, he learned to grip onto the sledge so tightly that even hurtling across banks and ridges of snow and swirling about slopes of ice, he kept his hold; only a violent shock against some jutting object could pitch him overboard. There was so much to learn if he was to survive the ordeal of a long polar trek. But Cook learnt fast, burrowing like the Eskimos into a snow drift during a storm and keeping only a breathing hole open over his face, for as long as twenty-eight hours.

By the time winter was over, Cook had shown that he did not balk at any of the dangers that the Eskimos faced. He would never be as competent as them but he had grasped all that they had tried to teach. He had trodden the same route in winter to the walrus hunting grounds – a journey of 500 miles (800 kilometres) in the dark when the orange glow of the sun gave way to eerie blackness; when the dogs tumbled, jumped and raced over broken pack-ice; and when they squirmed and snaked their way over dangerously thin ice. He had felt despair and fear as he twisted through glaciers gashed and broken by bottomless canyons, where a false step might plunge him to his death; and he had survived to witness the climax of the hunter's vigil, when with raised arm and sudden thrust, the hunter delivered the harpoon into the vitals of his beast of prey.

When February arrived Cook was almost ready – his long initiation was over and he was prepared to lead the greatest expedition of his life. He had long since planned his route, which would lead first westward and then northward, away from the 'American Route' that Peary intended to follow.

Annoatok was 700 miles (1,120 kilometres) from the Pole

but as Cook admitted, those 700 miles would stretch to 1,000 with all the detours that would be necessary. In all, he would have to travel a minimum of 2,000 miles (3,210 kilometres). On the morning of 19 February 1908 Dr Frederick Cook set out. He was accompanied by Francke, nine Eskimos and 103 dogs. Men and dogs had fed abundantly on walrus meat for several weeks and they were all in good fettle.

The sun rose for the first time on 20 February, but it gave no warmth, and during the next few weeks they suffered frostbitten faces and burns from handling the metal on the guns. The temperatures were low, dropping to −83°F (−64°C). The marches were exhausting, as much of the time the men had to run to keep from getting too cold – one dog froze to death.

Francke turned back with some of the Eskimos, with instructions to look after Cook's provisions until the time came for him to get a ship home; and Cook went on with two Eskimos, Etukishook and Ahwelah, young men only twenty years old.

Cook's route lay across Smith Sound to Cape Sabine, and from there across Ellesmere Island to the west coast, as far as the northernmost tip of Axel Heiberg Island. It was territory offering the most game and Cook was anxious to keep his expedition provisions intact for that part of the journey that lay across the sea-ice.

They used twenty-six of the best dogs, and Cook planned that twenty of them would be used one by one as food for the others. Every unnecessary fibre of wood was gouged out of the sledges, as Cook reported; even the iron runners were filed down. Along the way, a large cache was left in case they had used up all their food by the time they returned.

In less than a month they covered 400 miles (645 kilometres), fighting their way through deep snows on land, and mountainous, frozen seas; and when they reached Cape Thomas Hubbard, the northernmost tip of Axel Heiberg Island, Cook looked out over the 'fields of crushed ice glimmering in the rising sunlight with shooting fires of sapphire and green' and felt exalted. Fields of ice, churned by strong currents into jagged mountainous heaps, stretched to the horizon, but he was now 520 miles (836 kilometres) from the Pole.

For days he and his two companions hacked their way through jumbled walls of ice, penetrating deeper and still deeper into the polar pack – a place of storms and mists, of treacherous ice and dazzling mirages. The desire to increase the miles between them and land turned almost to panic when the Eskimos eventually lost sight of it altogether, and throughout the wearisome trek Cook had to encourage them to continue by pretending that the low-lying clouds on the horizon were indeed signs of land. This very deception was to make Cook's detractors claim that he could not have reached the Pole.

As the days passed, the men pushed and pulled the overloaded sledges, spending much time climbing hummocks to look for the easiest route in the direction they wished to go. Hours were spent chopping their way through the enormous barriers of ice.

At the end of each gruelling day they made camp by building an igloo – a dome-shaped snow house. On one occasion, as the air thickened with blowing snow, they recognized the signs of an approaching hurricane, and to protect themselves, they built a double snow wall on the wind side of the igloo. Although they poured water over the snow to cement the blocks together, the wind still burrowed small holes through the walls and let in the suffocating drift.

In the lull that followed this storm they slept, only to be woken by terrifying sounds coming from beneath the ice as if from a huge explosion. For a while nothing happened and all seemed tranquil, but as suddenly the commotion began again, and Cook, caught in his sleeping bag, felt a sensation of being at sea in a tossing ship. Unable to move and 'with a suffocating sense of falling' he felt a lightening pressure around him 'like that of a chilled and closing shell of steel, driving the life and breath' from him. The ice had cracked open beneath the igloo and he was floundering in the icy water surrounded by tumbling blocks of snow and ice. Fortunately his companions, who had managed to leap to safety, acted quickly and just saved him from an icy death.

The closer they got to the Pole, the more wretched conditions became – cold and hunger tormented them and the need to economize on fuel prevented their melting the ice to satisfy their craving thirst. They survived on two meals a day, their food being pemmican or frozen meat. Time, food and fuel were short – there were no stops for lunch, no place to ride on the overloaded sledges, no rest, only the awful necessity to drive themselves further and further.

Ice accumulated on their faces as the moisture from their breath condensed and froze. It covered their eyelashes and brows and formed icicles on the hairs within their nostrils. Dogs and men were driving themselves to the limit, and when the dogs could take no more, they were fed to their companions.

The desolate world around them froze their spirits. Cook admitted he 'felt the tragic isolation of the human soul – a thing which, dwelt upon, must mean madness. I think I realized the aching vastness of the world after creation, before man was made.' Theirs was the loneliness of being 'alone in a lifeless world'.

When they were just over 100 miles (160 kilometres) from the Pole one of the Eskimos broke down. Dispirited and frightened at the signs of an oncoming storm, he told Cook he could not go on, and that all he wanted was to die. For the Eskimos, who never hunted out of sight of land, the Arctic Ocean was a bewildering, unfriendly place. For them the North Pole held no magic, and they felt they had gone far enough in this useless quest. What benefit could be gained by reaching it? Cook reasoned gently with the Eskimos, encouraging them with the news that only a few more days should see them there, and pointing to the mirages on the horizon which, Cook told the Eskimos, were land.

As they neared the Pole, their shadows at night shortened, until one day there seemed no difference in the length of their shadows throughout the whole day. The Eskimos were confused by this, but Cook told them that this was because they were at the North Pole. Any further explanation was difficult, because Cook did not know enough Eskimo to go into any scientific detail.

The excitement of reaching the North Pole Cook describes as something which 'thrilled through his nerves and veins like the shivering sound of silver bells'. Fortunately for him then, he had no inkling that his great competitor, Robert Peary, was to rob him of that glory. 21 April 1908 was the date Cook claimed to have reached the North Pole. During the two days they remained at the Pole, Cook took systematic observations to fix his position. Victory felt sweet, but the urgent need to get back and tell the world, before starvation or the ice claimed them, made them hurry to return.

Food was low, owing to delays when they had been holed up during storms. The ice would soon be breaking up and melting, and if they were unlucky they might be prevented by open water from reaching land.

The race home was even more dramatic than their struggle towards the Pole – for twenty days mist blinded them, while they drifted in a direction they could not tell. Weakened by hunger and cold, the spectre of a lingering death from starvation loomed up to haunt them.

Many were the perils of their return, but none more dramatic than the occasion, in Jones Sound, when they took refuge from the churning pack on an iceberg. They harnessed themselves to it by ropes as it 'ploughed its way through the miles of sea-ice, crushing it and throwing it aside'. Suddenly it turned at right angles to its course and battered its way out of the pack into the seething sea. Huge waves washed over them and would have knocked them from their footing had not the freezing water frozen their feet to the berg. For twenty-four hours they struggled to hold on till a chance came for them, in a tranquil moment, to leap to the safety of their portable canoe. By now all their dogs were gone.

With great hardship and suffering they eventually reached Cape Sparbo, where they found an ancient Eskimo village half sunk into the ground. They were 300 miles (480 kilometres) from Annoatok and it was now early September. With ammunition low, they had had to improvise some kind of weapons to kill game, from bits of sledge and from bones from old carcasses. Anyone less courageous would have given up the struggle long before, but Cook and his two Eskimo companions were remarkable men. Where their primitive weapons failed them they used cunning – competing with the polar bear for the same food. Too often the bear beat them to it, and even when the men managed to kill a walrus and cache the meat, the polar bears raided their cache. But the men managed to survive. They laid in a stock of meat for the winter and for a hundred days retreated to their den beneath the ground.

Never had they felt so isolated and alone, surrounded as they were by 'satanic blackness' and marauding bears. They schooled themselves to be patient and on 11 February 1909 burst out of their prison to freedom. It was 18 April 1909

before Cook and his companions did eventually reach Annoatok. They had had a terrible trek through territory far from
the haunts of game and in desperation they had eaten bits of
old boots and tough walrus lines made from strips of hide.

The joy of returning to his friends was overshadowed by
the news that Peary had confiscated all Cook's belongings.
However, Cook did not wait to brood. Bidding his companions tell Peary when they saw him that Cook had only
travelled a short distance and never went out of sight of
land – he journeyed south to catch a boat back to civilization.
Something cautioned him not to tell Peary of his victory
until he had had time to cable the news of his success to the
world.

Sadly the news of Cook's triumph, sent from Lerwick in
the Shetland Islands, unleashed a chain of disastrous events
for him. Peary called him a liar, and from that moment a
bitter dispute began which has lasted even up to the present
day. Peary supporters jumped to the call to defend their
hero – moneyed and influential, as many of them were, they
organized a network of intrigue to discredit the Doctor.

Cook had left his charts and figures in Annoatok in the
charge of a visiting American sportsman, Harry Whitney,
who offered to bring them back with him to America, since
Cook's journey south promised to be hazardous. But Peary
refused to let Whitney bring the documents aboard, and hid
them – they were never found again. Cook's Eskimos faith-
fully testified that they had always been in sight of land,
although they admitted travelling out onto the sea-ice for
seven moons and reaching a place where the sun did not dip
at night, and where day and night shadows were of equal
length. Peary chose to believe the first part of their statement
and ignored the rest.

Cook's description of the region surrounding the North
Pole 'where there was no land, only the polar ice-pack in a

state of continuous motion and upheaval' was original and has been verified not only by Peary, but by other explorers.

The battle grew more and more vindictive and Cook, sickened by the injustice and meanness of the fight, withdrew from the arena. But his enemies would not let him rest, and a vicious newspaper campaign had its effect. In no time the man whom everyone had fêted in the first days of his return became a scapegoat for all kinds of abuse. Robbed of his honour, he fell foul of the law and was imprisoned for fraud. He had entered the business of real estate and was convicted of selling worthless land on the understanding that it was rich in oil. Ironically he served seven years in prison while those to whom he had sold the land amassed a fortune from it. No one came to bail him out.

Much has been written about this mild, unassuming physician – a great deal of it untrue – but even a cursory look at the record of his early expeditions shows him to be courageous and competent. Perhaps the best testimony to Cook is that of Roald Amundsen, with whom Cook served on the Belgica Expedition, in the Antarctic: 'He was beloved and respected by all . . . upright, capable and conscientious in the extreme. He of all the ship's company, was the one man of unfaltering courage, unfailing hope, endless cheerfulness and unwearied kindness . . . His ingenuity and enterprise were boundless . . . The success of the whole Belgian expedition was due to him.'

Commander Peary claimed he reached the North Pole on 9 April 1909

The *Endurance*, keeled over, was abandoned a few days
before being crushed by the ice

A group of huskies watch as the *Endurance* is crushed
after nine months in the ice

Fridtjof Nansen, drawn after a photograph taken by
Frederick Jackson on the day of their meeting

Mawson peering into the crevasse for signs of his sledge companion Ninnis who had fallen through the fragile crevasse bridge

On the march after leaving the *Jeannette*: drawn from minute descriptions by Lieutenant Danenhower

The Chilean tug *Yelcho* comes to the relief of the stranded men of Shackleton's party, 6 August 1916

Wally Herbert lights his pipe during a sledging break on the British Trans-Arctic Expedition.(*below*) One of the expedition's dog teams

The last great journey on Earth
Herbert

(The author is married to Wally Herbert, the subject of this adventure)

There is now hardly an acre on the surface of the earth which has not been photographed from the air or trodden by the foot of man, but when Wally Herbert, at the age of twenty-one, went to the Antarctic in 1955, three-quarters of the continent still remained to be explored. In the four years Herbert spent in the Antarctic he mapped 45,000 square miles, but even as he was doing this, time and territory were running out as aerial surveys took up the task. There still remained his ambition to sledge to the South Pole, but by now an American Base had been established there and permission was refused for the young man to satisfy his personal dream.

His work in the Antarctic finished, Wally looked to the north for a way to realize his ambition to make a long polar journey. A map of the Arctic Ocean caught his attention; on it were marked the Russian scientific stations which had been established on ice-floes. Looking closer he realized that they had drifted and that the tracks of the drift had been plotted on the map. Excited by this observation, he added to these markings the tracks of the American scientific drifting stations and the drift of the *Fram* (the first ship to cross the Arctic Ocean). An interesting fact emerged. He noticed that the ice circulated in a pattern which was broadly divided into two currents. This gave him an idea. Maybe a party of men and dog teams could take advantage of the

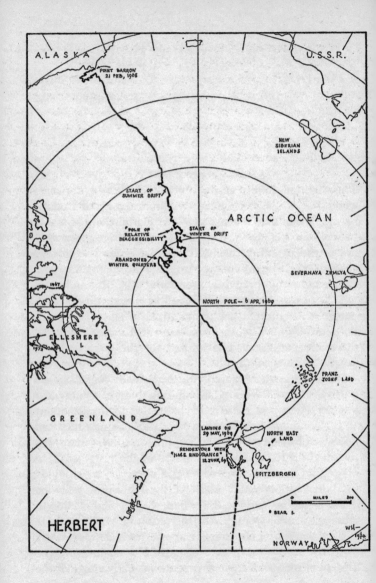

current to cross the whole of the Arctic Ocean, via the Pole, from one side to the other!

The more he thought about the idea the more it appealed to him. Here was a big journey – in both time and distance – for he calculated that it would take sixteen months to cross from Point Barrow in Alaska to North-east Greenland or Spitzbergen; a distance of 1,850 airline miles, which when added to the detours necessary, would amount to 3,800 actual miles (6,115 kilometres).

Obviously four men could not carry on four sledges enough food, clothing and equipment to last them for sixteen months; supporting parties like Peary's were out of the question because of the distance, as was the idea of using a ship like the *Fram*, as Nansen had done. No – the only way was to use the old technique of dog sledging backed up by modern aircraft support.

For the next five years Wally threw himself into the business of organizing the expedition. They were five years of hard work, frustration and many disappointments. Only the thought of the courage and pride of the polar heroes he so much admired kept him from losing all faith. Critics were sceptical not only of the feasibility of the plan but of the value of such an expensive and hazardous undertaking.

After a training journey in North-west Greenland, living with the Eskimos for nine months to learn their techniques of travel and survival, Wally led an expedition across Ellesmere Island to Resolute Bay. So successful was this trip that his critics admitted he was the right man for the job. In the training programme Wally and his two companions had crossed 1,500 miles (2,414 kilometres) of inhospitable country, retracing Cook's outward journey to the Pole across Ellesmere Island and Axel Heiberg Island. He had driven his two companions and himself to the absolute limit of their endurance, to see if they would be capable of the longer journey across the Arctic Ocean. They had very nearly died of starvation, but they had proved themselves ready for the greater test.

There have to be very good reasons for wanting to cross the Arctic Ocean, apart from getting to the other side. There was tremendous scope for scientific work to be done on the expedition: synoptic weather observations, and studies of ice, of the distribution of wild life in the central Arctic Basin, and of survival techniques, which would be made available to airline companies operating air routes over the North Pole.

The date set for departure from Barrow was 1 February 1968. The weeks before had been full of activity, training the dogs and getting the stores and equipment sorted out. Herbert had decided to divide the journey into five phases – three periods of sledging, when they would be able to counter any adverse drift of ice, and two periods – the height of summer when much of the ice would melt, and the long polar winter when darkness would make travelling impossible – when they would be completely at the mercy of the drift. A tight schedule of distances to be travelled by certain dates had to be worked out – and the success or failure of the expedition would depend on how accurately Wally could predict the drift and how closely they could keep to the schedule. Throughout the journey there would be seven airdrops.

The four men who were to make the journey were Wally Herbert himself, Allan Gill, Fritz Koerner and Dr Kenneth Hedges. A fifth man, Squadron-Leader Freddie Church, was to remain at Barrow to provide a direct radio link between the expedition and the Royal Aircraft Establishment's experimental radio station at Farnborough. At a certain stage in the expedition the fifth member was to move to the American Ice Island in the Arctic Ocean in order to be nearer the expedition.

1 February arrived but they could not leave. Between Barrow and the polar pack lay an 80-mile (128-kilometre) gap of young ice which was impossible to cross. Usually this belt of fractured ice was still and packed tight for three weeks during this period, but this year there seemed no chance of its settling down. For days the party waited, their nerves taut, as the ice jostled and grated along the coast, separating into smoking seas of open water. Ice drifting at two knots or more worked itself like slime across the water and, like slime, it was incapable of bearing any weight. While the Eskimos in Barrow plotted with crosses on the map the places where the expedition members would be likely to meet their deaths, the hopes of the British Trans-Arctic Expedition were beginning to crumble. They needed a gentle wind to tap the floes together to form a single skin for a headlong dash, but even then the possibilities of a change of weather splitting the fragile crust, with the inevitable consequences, could not be ignored.

At last they got their chance on 21 February. Air reconnaissance showed a highway of clear ice stretched to a point some 60 miles (96 kilometres) to the east of Barrow, from which they could make a dash across the 80-mile (130-kilometre) belt of fractured ice.

The relief the men felt on completing the distance due east was shattered when they clambered the wall of jumbled ice to get a look towards the north. A chaos of ice met their gaze in every direction except the way they had come. Desperate as the situation was they could not turn back; to have done so would have meant to abandon the expedition – it was already late in the season, and any more delays and they would not be able to complete their schedules and might pay the penalty for delay with their deaths.

They took up their ice-axes and hacked a bite out of the wall – it took two hours to clear a way and to build a ramp on either side with the debris for the dogs and sledges to get through. Within three hours, sweating and hoarse from screaming at the dogs, they had crossed their first ice ridge – ahead of them, before the end of their journey, they would have to cross another twenty thousand of these obstacles.

For days the fate of the men hung in the balance. Camping on a fragile skin of ice, stumbling across broken floes, sinking into an icy porridge and fleeing from mountains of pressure which ate up the ice behind them, they desperately struggled from one hazard to another. All around them the ice was cracking and disintegrating; the drift was drawing them back towards Barrow, and with fear and despair they realized they could smell the sea. The hours of daylight were short; it was the coldest time of the year and the expedition was in a perilous position. The strain was telling on the men. Even when, for a while, the surface improved, they found travelling on the ice was like being on a treadmill. The miles covered during the day were lost overnight in drifting when they were asleep. Sleep, however, was fitful and never lasted more than four or five hours – they were tense and anxious, listening for the cracks in the ice, cracks that crept like black snakes towards their tent, and which if they reached them would have dropped them into the sea.

By 18 March they were out of the fractured zone – 400 miles (640 kilometres) behind schedule and 1,170 miles (1,872 kilometres) from the Pole. Ahead of them was a long monotonous haul. So expert did they become at travelling that they could scramble over walls of icy rubble as it was heaving under their feet, and they could balance delicately on ice that wobbled like a jelly when they planted a foot on it. But even so, some areas they covered sprang into motion and could only be crossed in a headlong rush as they drove the dogs with screams and cracking whips. Herbert recalls these moments of exciting scrambles as 'tense, dangerous and hot as hell'.

By 10 May they had sledged about 900 miles (1,440 kilometres) across vast areas of ice barely thick enough to support the weight of a sledge – areas which only a few days before had been seas of open water. Three dogs had been lost out of the original forty, but the remainder seemed in good condition. The sledges, on the other hand, were splitting and falling apart and only relashing and a careful application of splints could hold them together. The men, too, were weatherworn, tired and limping.

In mist the party struggled through a maze of shattered floes, converting the sledges to boats to ferry dogs and gear across the lanes of water. At times the men sank up to their thighs in slush. They were now fighting for every mile, as all around them the summer melt ate up the ice on which they moved. Currents and counter-currents stirred the floes into whirlpools which carried the men off-course to the east. Hungry tongues of water licked the edges of the floes, and gaping black mouths opened between the ice, waiting to devour them. Desperately they tried to move north-west to find a big enough floe on which to camp during the summer melt. Time was running out and if they did not find it soon they would sink, like stones, through the melting surface beneath.

On 3 July, wading through slush and icy water up to their knees, they set up camp on a hummocky old floe 'which stretched to the horizon like a vast, dazzling sheet'. In ten days' time the Canadian Air Force was scheduled to drop food to last them through the summer, together with various scientific instruments. To Wally's horror he found there was a break in the generator cable that fed the radio batteries. Nothing could be more serious than a radio breakdown. In five million square miles of ice there would be no way a man from the air could spot them – the homing beacons were only of marginal value. The fate of the whole expedition depended on getting the cable mended. Fortunately Allan was very skilful and with a makeshift soldering iron, he managed to do the necessary repair in time for the airdrop.

The camp was called 'Meltville', and for the whole of the summer the party followed their various scientific programmes. It was a restful but depressing time – fogs blanketed the floes, the men were wet with the drizzle from above and the melt beneath. But it gave Wally an opportunity to finalize his plans for the next stages. On leaving the summer camp they would need to push hard for the north before finding a good floe for the winter camp.

On 4 September they set off with heavy loads across treacherous surfaces; a few days later Allan slipped a disc in a bad fall. There was no alternative but to return to their old floe to sit out the winter drift. More supplies were airdropped later in the month, together with a prefabricated hut in which they were to drift throughout the long, dark months of winter.

The 28 tons of food, fuel and equipment were scattered around the floe which was by then only 2 kilometres (just over a mile) in diameter. All around were smaller floes covering an area of about 13 square kilometres (5 square miles). It was hard and exhausting work sorting out the newly dropped supplies and stacking them so that they would be easy to get at. They had no sooner finished the job than the floe cracked up like an eggshell. In frantic haste the men dismantled the hut, hampered by darkness and widening cracks, which threatened to spill them and their supplies into the sea. In a perilous race they relayed the hut and their mountainous supplies to a site 2 kilometres (just over a mile) away, where they stayed for the rest of the winter.

With the new year, the men were impatient to be on the

move. The journey ahead seemed impossible – in one hundred days they had to travel the distance they had covered in a year in order to reach Spitzbergen ahead of the melt season. They would have to abandon winter quarters three weeks ahead of sunrise, and force-march for the remainder of the journey, carrying all the exposed film, some scientific instruments and the massive amount of data. They would be sledging across the drift, and would therefore have to travel as light as possible. In other words the final airdrop would have to be divided into three, to enable them to make a dash for Spitzbergen.

On 24 February, the day they were scheduled to set off, the floe shattered. Fortunately Allan was not in his tent when the crack went right under it, or he would not have survived – he had been sleeping in the tent most of the winter. All hell broke loose as the men scrambled to collect their gear and haul it outside before the ice broke up beneath them. Armed with sheath knives in case they had to cut themselves free, they worked like demons, knowing that their lives hung by a rapidly fraying cord.

Tumbling out into the blackness of the night, they jumped and scrambled over heaving pressure and parting lanes of water to reach the dogs which were howling and whimpering, sensing their danger on the jostling floes. Racing for their lives, they sledged northwards to the darkest part of the horizon, with only Venus as a guide. Fortunately for them, Allan by now was in good shape.

On 6 April 1969 they reached the Pole, sixty years after Peary claimed he reached it. From now on their journey lay south, 'straight down the Greenwich meridian towards home'.

As the ice improved, a new danger threatened their lives. One day Herbert was at the back of the line of sledges when he sensed something behind him. Looking round, he found he was being stalked by a polar bear. The situation was dangerous. The rifle on his sledge had not been adequately degreased; consequently it was liable to seize up. Apart from this, the nearest ammunition was in his anorak which he had, that morning, stuffed inside the load at the front of the sledge.

The dogs had not sensed the bear. They were puzzled by Herbert's frantic yells to get a move on and kept looking around. Meanwhile the bear was closing in. The only chance was to crawl along the moving sledge and dig out the anorak. The seconds seemed like minutes as Wally inched his way on his belly towards the front of the sledge. Feverishly he tugged at the ropes to unleash the gear. Delving inside, he fished out the anorak and rummaged for the bullets. The bear was less than 50 yards (45 metres) away. Sitting astride the load, Wally fed four rounds into the rifle and rammed one up the spout. The rifle would not fire and while Wally wrestled with the bolt, the bear hurried forward excitedly. In desperation, Wally hit the bolt with the palm of his hand and the rifle fired. It was not aimed at the bear, but the noise stopped it in its tracks. By the time the dog team had extended the gap to 100 yards (90 metres), the bear seemed to lose interest and ambled off.

As they neared land the bears became more frequent and more menacing. It was too dangerous to sleep in tents in case a bear attacked. The men had to sleep on the sledges with a rifle beside them so that at the first whine from the dogs they could be ready. From now on the sledges were arranged in the centre of the camp with the dogs on the perimeter to give the men time to respond to the dogs' warning before the bear attacked.

On 23 May, land was sighted – Phipps Island, one of the Svalbard group. A wide belt of jostling ice guarded its shores – ice more dangerous than any they had yet set foot on. The danger in crossing that ice, even should it compact tightly for a short while, was great; but the risk had to be taken if the journey was to have any significance. Already they were late in the season – HMS *Endurance* was now on standby and there was no possibility of reaching Spitzbergen itself before the ice broke up. They must make for the nearest land.

Marooned for hours on a floe, they waited like cats watching a mouse for the ice to close in. On 29 May their moment came. The ice they were on was knitted to the rest of the jumbled mass in a rough skin reaching the shore of a small, rocky island called Tavløya. Ken Hedges and Allan Gill were given the privilege of scrambling ashore to bring back a chunk of granite to prove their claim. With their landfall, the long haul was over; they could triumphantly rendezvous with the ship waiting to take them home.

At the moment when man was setting foot on the Moon for the first time, the British Trans-Arctic Expedition was completing its journey. In sixteen months it had crossed 3,720 miles (5,986 kilometres) of treacherous pack-ice. It had been the longest sustained sledging journey in the whole history of polar exploration. It had completed successfully the first surface-crossing of the Arctic Ocean, a feat of endurance and courage which ranks with the greatest journeys of exploration: in fact this must surely be the last great journey on Earth.

The Arctic today

No longer is the Arctic inaccessible. The Eskimos who fringe the shores of the Arctic Ocean have long since learned that they are not the only people in the world – a belief which made them call themselves the Inuit, 'the People', to differentiate between themselves and the animals they hunted. Now every year, people flock to the Arctic, anthropologists to study the Eskimos, and conservationists to study the environment. In a world suffering from the effects of over-population and over-exploitation of resources, the Arctic holds the solution to some of the problems.

Nowadays, airline companies make regular flights over the North Pole. Russian and American scientists man the ice stations established on drifting floes and ice islands in the Arctic Ocean. Even the waters beneath the ice have been penetrated: in 1958, an American nuclear submarine, the *Nautilus*, dived beneath the ice near Point Barrow and after searching with echo-sounding gear, found the required ocean depth in which to begin its journey beneath the ice of the Arctic Ocean towards Spitzbergen on the other side.

Strategically, the Arctic is of vital importance to all of us, because facing each other across the Arctic Ocean are two of the world's great powers – Russia and North America; and scattered around the Arctic are Distant Early Warning stations fitted with sophisticated electronic detectors to enable us to be prepared in the event of a sudden missile attack.

We have now acquired the technique of living in the far north, and even now, vast sums of money are being spent in Canada and Alaska to siphon off the oil which so many of us need. But progress brings problems; and the greatest problem is the danger of destroying the quality of life for the Eskimos in order to create a better quality of life for ourselves. For if our pipe-laying machines destroy too much of the tundra – that thin covering of delicate plant life and mossy soil that covers the permanently frozen ground in the Arctic – then a whole cycle of life would be destroyed. For the tundra supplies food to the reindeer which in turn supplies food to man. Fortunately, the oil companies are aware of this and hopefully they will find the right solution to the problem.

2 The Antarctic explorers

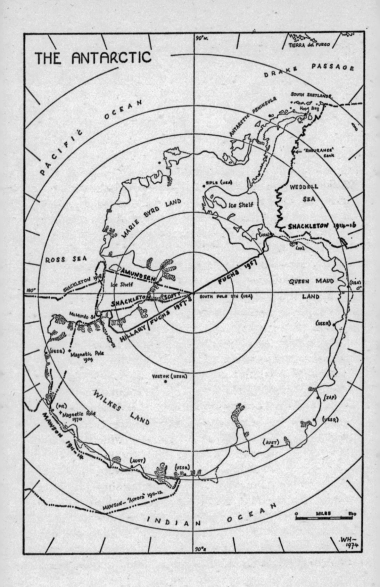

Introduction

While explorers in the north painstakingly filled in the blanks on their maps and found that the Arctic was an ocean, not a land mass, a huge continent of virgin land lay waiting to be discovered at the opposite end of the earth, at the South Pole.

For centuries it had existed in the minds of geographers: the early Greeks, obsessed with the necessity for balance and symmetry in nature, concluded that the 'excess of land in the northern hemisphere must be balanced by a land mass in the southern hemisphere'.

When Magellan sailed completely round the world, proving that the earth was a sphere, his account of land round Tierra del Fuego sent cartographers scurrying to their maps to pencil in 'Terra Australis' – a huge imaginary land mass, which covered an enormous part of the southern hemisphere representing an area of over ten million square miles (twenty-five million square kilometres) which extended nearly as far north as Cape Horn and the Cape of Good Hope, and which included the still undiscovered Australia.

As more and more explorers took to their ships, it became evident that the huge land mass represented on the maps was a myth. Bit by bit, portions of the continent were lopped off, as men sailed farther and farther south. The map-makers could not keep up with the constantly changing boundaries which forced them to rub out old borders and pencil in new ones. It was a cartographer's nightmare which made some of them so sick of the whole business that they wiped the troublesome continent completely off their maps.

In 1773 Captain James Cook crossed the Antarctic Circle; on his return two years later he expressed his belief that an Antarctic continent probably existed, but added that it was inaccessible because of the barrier of ice that surrounded it.

It took an Englishman, James Clark Ross, the most experienced Arctic explorer of his day and age, to penetrate the Antarctic pack with the ships *Erebus* and *Terror* in 1840. He discovered Victoria Land, named two volcanoes Erebus and Terror, and sailed parallel to the Great Ice Barrier. Now called the Ross Ice Shelf, this is a vast apron of ice locked to the inland ice and stretching out to sea, an area larger in size than the whole of France. He did not reach the South Magnetic Pole as he had hoped – it was impossible to reach this by sea – but he opened up the icy world of the Antarctic; and it was from the area that he discovered that the great British journeys towards the South Pole were to be launched some fifty years later.

Forestalled:
Scott

It was a lucky day for the young Lieutenant of His Majesty's Navy, on leave from his ship, when he met Sir Clements Markham, the President of the Royal Geographical Society, while walking in London. The two men had met some years before and Markham had been most impressed with Lieutenant Robert Falcon Scott's 'intelligence and charm of manner'.

The younger man crossed the street to show courtesy to Markham, and then accompanied him to his house. In the course of that afternoon Sir Clements Markham unfolded his plan to send an expedition to the Antarctic, to explore the coast and the inland ice of that unknown continent. His words fired the imagination of his young listener, and when Sir Clements announced that the privilege of undertaking this mission should belong to the Navy, young Scott decided he would apply for the leadership himself.

It is doubtful if Scott would have been interested in polar exploration had he not met Sir Clements that afternoon. He certainly admitted having had no previous ambition to become a polar explorer. But however ordinary his aspirations before that meeting, he came out of it with a new purpose to his life. He was accepted for the position of leader and a year later was promoted to commander.

No time was lost preparing the great expedition. A specially designed ship, the *Discovery*, was built to withstand

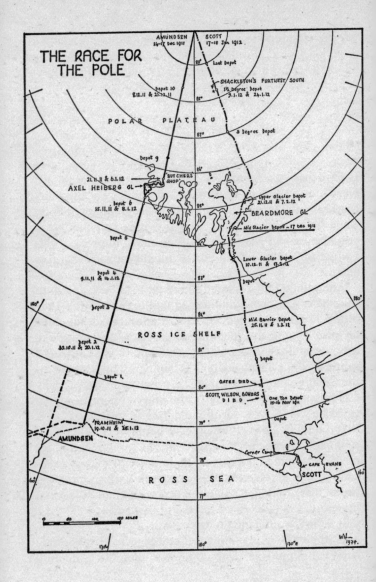

the ice, and in August 1901 she set sail for the Antarctic. The discoveries on this expedition were remarkable – hundreds of miles of coast were explored and the features recorded. Various mountain ranges were discovered and named, and Scott and his party had the privilege of being the first to sledge across the great ice shelf, which surrounds the land mass of the Antarctic.

Accompanying Scott on this expedition was a young merchant seaman called Ernest Shackleton. An outstanding personality and an ability to turn his hand to any job he was asked to do won for Shackleton the admiration of Scott and the affection of Dr Edward Wilson, Scott's greatest friend. It was largely due to Wilson that Shackleton was chosen, in spite of Scott's preference for naval men, to accompany him and Wilson on their next exploit – the first inland journey of exploration towards the South Pole.

Although the men used dogs to haul their sledges, they were not experienced dog drivers, and the animals were often more trouble than they were worth. (There can be nothing more exasperating than a team of undisciplined huskies. They fight amongst each other, twisting their traces into impossibly complicated tangles, and generally do the opposite to what you want them to do.)

The expedition reached 82°17' S, just 540 miles (870 kilometres) from the South Pole, before they were forced to turn back, weakened by cold and lack of food. One by one the dogs collapsed and were fed to the others. The men suffered dreadfully from an ill-balanced diet and scurvy soon set in, affecting Shackleton the worst. Shackleton was unable to pull his weight, and it is a great credit to his two companions that he was brought through alive.

When they returned to base they found the relief ship awaiting them, and Scott decided Shackleton should be invalided home on this while the others remained to continue their explorations. Scott's decision was not only to destroy the warm relationship between the two men, but was to create a rivalry which would last until Scott's death.

Humiliated at being sent home, Shackleton vowed to return and take the Pole himself. His recovery back in England was quick and he set about preparing for his own expedition. He was unwilling to announce his venture until he was sure of his plans, and until he knew he could raise the money to pay for it, but by 1906 he felt he could safely leak the news. He proposed, he said, to lead an expedition to the Antarctic with its two main objectives to reach the South Pole and the South Magnetic Pole.

The South Pole is a fixed point on the earth's surface where all the lines of longitude in the Southern Hemisphere meet – it is the southern axis of the earth – in other words, it is the southern tip of the imaginary rod running through the earth from north to south, on which the earth spins. The South Magnetic Pole, on the other hand, is the point on the earth's surface where all the magnetic lines of force converge. It is constantly shifting, and it is almost 1,500 miles (2,414 kilometres) from the South Pole itself, being near the coast of the continent. It became of great interest to explorers in the nineteenth century, when many of the wooden ships were replaced by those built with iron. This posed problems of navigation which had not been important before. The magnetic compass points to the Magnetic Pole and not to the Geographic Pole. In the days of Shackleton, and even earlier, magnetic research was considered as important as meteorological investigations are today. Therefore, to bag both the South Pole and the South Magnetic Pole on one expedition would indeed be a prize.

It was some time before Scott was informed of the announcement because at the time Shackleton made it, Scott was in the Atlantic in command of HMS *Albemarle*. The news shocked him, as he had set his heart on making another attempt for the Pole, and although he had made no firm plans and had not even fixed a date for his expedition, the emergence of a competitor was something he could not have foreseen. Jealous of the area which he regarded as his own, Scott extracted a promise from Shackleton that he would not launch his expedition from the vicinity of McMurdo Sound – the base that Scott had used for his first expedition.

As circumstances turned out, Shackleton had no alternative but to winter at the site of his former expedition – although he put himself at great risk in an attempt to find another suitable location. It was a bitter pill for Scott to swallow when he heard that Shackleton had sledged to within 97 nautical miles (180 kilometres) of the South Pole, before being forced by lack of food to turn back on 9 January 1909.

It is difficult to get an accurate picture of Scott without appearing to be contradictory. On the one hand he was described by his friends as peevish, highly strung and moody, while on the other he was described as a sensitive person with a tremendous sense of justice and a charm unlike any other human being. His magnetic personality drew loyalty and love from those who served with him, and whatever his mistakes, and he made several on his last expedition, he had the gift to inspire men to such an extent that they were prepared to lay down their lives for him.

Ten thousand men, most of them Army or Navy officers, applied to join Scott's new South Polar Expedition, of whom less than a hundred were chosen! They soon fell under Scott's spell as they listened to his tales of the stormy southern seas, the mystery of the Great Ice Barrier (The Ross Ice Shelf), the grandeur of the mountains and the marvels of the animal life teeming in the surrounding cold waters.

Many scientific subjects were to be studied, but public interest and Scott's cherished dream lay in the intended dash for the Pole. Scott had resigned himself to the disappointment of retracing over 400 miles (650 kilometres) of Shackleton's route towards the Pole, but another shock was awaiting him which would have a far more disastrous effect. At Melbourne, on his way down south, he received a telegram from Roald Amundsen, a famous Norwegian explorer with the message that he was going south. This could mean only one thing – the Norwegian was also to make a try for the Pole.

Ironically, the base in which the Norwegians chose to winter was the Bay of Whales – a sheltered place Scott had discovered when he had set out to find the eastern limit of the Ross Ice Shelf. Amundsen was to use dogs for the journey, while Scott had decided on a combination of three types of transport for the initial stages, followed by a system of manhauling for the final stages. Scott had Siberian ponies, motor toboggans and two dog teams, and it has been considered by many explorers that his greatest mistake was not to have used dogs all the way.

Dogs, when handled well, are a very efficient way of travelling in the polar regions, but Scott had an aversion to using them. He felt that the system of beating and whipping the dogs to get the best out of them was brutal. In part he was influenced by Sir Clements Markham – both men agreed that 'the conquest is more nobly and splendidly won' by man's unaided efforts than by forcing dogs to suffer. What they did not seem to realize is that a dog can pull almost as much as a man at twice the speed and for a much longer period of time.

Every expedition in the south spent the winter preparing for the journey it hoped to make when the sun returned. Scott was at a disadvantage because the ponies could not stand the cold as well as the dogs, and therefore he would have to delay his start by at least a month during the spring, in order that the animals would not suffer too much from the cold.

The route to the Pole from Scott's base can be seen in three stages: the first across the Ross Ice Shelf, the second up the Beardmore Glacier and the third across the Polar Plateau – a high, flat plain on which the South Pole is found at a level of approximately 10,000 feet (3,000 metres).

Scott's plan was to lay depots at intervals along the route and to use supporting parties for some of the way so that, from the last main depot, the Polar party could travel fairly lightly to the Pole and back. There were two great dangers in this system – firstly, if delayed by bad weather too long, the men might use up all their provisions long before reaching the next depot. Secondly, depots could be lost under drifts of snow. In either case, the result would be certain death.

The impatience Scott had felt while waiting to set out was only partly soothed by being actually on the march. Six ponies had been lost earlier while laying depots, and those that had survived to begin the great journey suffered terribly from the cold and the wind. They were difficult to handle, and when each had pulled to his limit, he was shot and the meat used to feed the men and the dogs. The motor toboggans broke down at the start, and only the dogs did the job satisfactorily.

Twelve miles (19 kilometres) from the Beardmore Glacier a howling blizzard broke. The men were unable to leave their tents for four days. Conditions were miserable as the snow melted beneath the tents, causing clothes and sleeping bags to become saturated. The falling snow melted on the ponies and then froze again on their backs and legs as the temperature dropped. Fodder soon ran out, and before long, all the ponies had to be shot and their meat cached for the return journey. Scott's men called the place Shambles Camp.

By 9 December they had been travelling for thirty-four days and were still 100 miles (160 kilometres) short of the point that Scott had hoped to reach by that date. Already Scott had broken into rations scheduled to be used on the plateau. It is not surprising that he felt depressed. The dogs turned back at the foot of the Beardmore Glacier, and from now on the men had to carry everything themselves.

The route now climbed for over 100 miles (160 kilometres) along glaciers. Ploughing at times through thick snow, relaying their loads over difficult patches, hacking through walls of ice, the men suffered agonies from snow blindness. Crevasses, some hidden by thin bridges of snow, others showing their ugly gaping mouths, made constant war on their nerves. On Christmas Day, Lashly fell through a bridge of snow and was only saved from plunging to his death by his harness, which was attached to the sledge.

Finally, on 4 January, about 150 miles (240 kilometres) from the Pole, the last supporting party turned back. Scott had planned to lead a four-man expedition on to the Pole, but at the last moment he decided to take another man. The implications of this decision were quite significant: rations and equipment had been made up for four men for five and a half weeks; however, five men would eat this in four weeks. There would be more discomfort in the four-man tent; cooking for five would take an hour longer during the day than cooking for four. An extra sleeping bag could make the sledge top-heavy and more liable to capsize in rough country. Five men were heavier on a crevasse lid than four. Finally, there were only four pairs of skis for five men, which meant that one person would be out of rhythm with the others, especially if he had to slog through soft snow. This could be a great strain on the fifth man.

It is easy to say that Scott should have realized this, and it is odd that no one challenged his decision. He said his farewells to his supporting party and turned towards the unknown with his four companions. No arrangements had been made for a party to relieve him, should he not return by a certain date; and he had no food to support him should he not keep to his schedule. As his supporting party turned back, he severed his last link with humanity.

Scott's four companions were Wilson, Bowers, Evans and Oates. For a while they advanced in good spirits although they found the going tough. A cold wind sucked the warmth from their aching bodies while scurvy sapped their strength.

Their spirits lifted as they passed Shackleton's farthest point south, but that joy was short-lived. Seven days later, on 16 January, they sighted a black flag and the tracks of dogs around the marks of a camp – Amundsen had been there. The Pole lay two days' march away but all pleasure had drained from the five men. They slogged on, but the sight of Amundsen's tent when they reached the Pole, containing a letter to Scott and a request to forward a letter to the King of Norway, was the ultimate disappointment.

The day was cold and miserable and the desolation of their location made Scott exclaim: 'Great God, this is an awful place and terrible enough for us to have laboured to it without the reward of priority.' Victory had been snatched from them, but what was more important to them now was the safety of their lives. Every minute wasted would count in the race to get back, before their food and strength gave out.

The return was a journey of monotony and torture. Food grew shorter and shorter, and the cold grew more and more unbearable as they lacked the strength and nutrition to fight it. Snow had drifted over their tracks and the surface became so difficult that they could barely pull their loads downhill. Seaman Evans showed the first signs of strain – he was bigger built than the others and needed more food to provide fuel for the greater energy he burned up; but the rations were already insufficient and each man received the same amount. He suffered terribly from frostbite on his hands and nose; eventually he died from a blow on the head which he got when he fell into a crevasse.

Soon all of them were suffering from falls amongst crevasses or from the cumulative effects of cold and hunger. Food had to be reduced because their exhausted condition took them longer to cover the distance. In attempts to catch up, they cut down on sleep, which only added to their misery and exhaustion.

At last Scott and his remaining three companions reached Shambles Camp, with its cache of food including some meat; but here a new worry arose as they discovered that fuel had leaked out from some of the cans.

The cold became even more intense, reaching sometimes 80 degrees of frost ($-62°C$) and their average daily march dropped to 5 or 6 miles (8 or 9 kilometres) instead of the minimum of 9 that they had allowed for their return. How soon would they run out of fuel?

By now Oates had become a drag on the party. The poor man had such swollen, frostbitten feet that he could barely move. He struggled bravely until he could go no further. In camp that night Scott asked Wilson to give them all opium pills in case they should have to take their own lives. They realized that Oates had reached the end of the road. Oates hoped he would die during the night; when morning came he decided he could no longer be a burden on his companions. Leaving the tent, he walked out into the wilderness and was seen no more.

In a desperate struggle Scott, Wilson and Bowers shortened the gap between themselves and their last depot –

One Ton Camp. On 19 March, just 11 miles (17 kilometres) from it, they made their final camp. They had two days' food left and barely a day's fuel. A blizzard blew up which confined them to their tent. It lasted ten days.

On 29 March Scott made his last entry in his diary. In a message he wrote to the public he ended up: 'Had we lived, I should have had a tale to tell of the hardihood, endurance, and courage of my companions which would have stirred the heart of every Englishman. These rough notes and our dead bodies must tell the tale.' They had travelled 1,646 miles (2,643 kilometres) and had been away from Base for 150 days. Now, just 11 miles from a life-saving supply of food, all were dead.

Eight months later they were found as they had died in their tent. A cairn was erected over them where they lay on the Ross Ice Shelf – the Great Ice Barrier that Scott had discovered was constantly on the move.

Many seasons have covered the spot with snow and it is no longer visible. But one day the piece of ice that has become his tomb will reach the end of the ice shelf – and there it will break off, like countless other icebergs, and Captain Scott, the naval officer, will return to the sea.

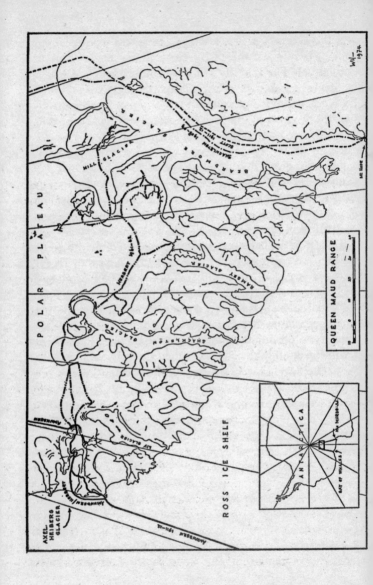

QUEEN MAUD RANGE

First at the Pole:
Amundsen

While Peary was still struggling across the pack-ice from the North Pole, a Norwegian explorer was working feverishly to complete his own preparations for a long polar expedition. Roald Amundsen, excited by the journeys that had been made in the north, determined to repeat the drift of the *Fram* (the first ship to drift with the ice across the Arctic Ocean) and when the ship was reasonably near the North Pole, he hoped to sledge towards it. His plans were almost complete when news broke of Peary's successful attempt at the North Pole. The dream of Amundsen was shattered – all his struggles had been in vain, all his organization counted for nothing.

In the depression that followed the news of Peary's success a ray of hope entered the Norwegian's spirit – why should he not go south ? If he could not have the North Pole what was to stop him from taking the South Pole ? The idea pleased him the more he thought about it and he made up his mind that that was what he would do. But disappointment had taught him a lesson. He had lost the race once, he must not lose again. Secrecy and speed were essential.

When Amundsen left Norway in August 1910, on the *Fram*, he had on board the best dog drivers and ski runners he could find. He had kept his change of plan from his sponsors and even from his crew. The ship would call at only one place on the way down south. Amundsen knew that Scott was also planning an attempt on the South Pole but he did not allow this to influence his decision. At Madeira, however, he had the courtesy to cable Scott who was then on his way to Melbourne, to tell him that he was going south.

Amundsen chose to winter at the Bay of Whales. His plan was to establish his base and then to lay depots as far to the south as possible before the winter set in. This plan was easily carried out with his shore parties laying depots as far as the 82nd Parallel. His depots were marked by snow beacons and the whole route well flagged. Amundsen's enterprise has been called 'one of the most perfect exhibitions of man's supremacy over the forces of nature'.

He spent the winter improving equipment and building up the strength of the men and dogs with plenty of fresh seal meat, to combat scurvy. He hoped to leave the station as early as possible in the spring – if they were to claim the record they 'must at any cost get there first'.

Scott's route up the Beardmore Glacier was 'without discussion declared out of bounds'. Amundsen hoped to pioneer a route 'from the Bay of Whales due south, following the same meridian, if possible, right up to the Pole'.

He had worked out his plans for crossing the 800 miles (1,280 kilometres) of unknown territory before he left Norway, and he predicted 'We shall be back from the polar journey on 25 January.' With this in mind, he set out with four companions and four sledges, each drawn by thirteen dogs in September 1911. Temperatures were so cold (−72°F, or −58°C) that they could not carry on, and caching all his food and equipment at latitude 80°, he returned to Base to wait for less cold weather. On 19 October he finally set out.

Although Amundsen's Base was a degree nearer the Pole than Scott's, he had the disadvantage of having to pioneer a new route. But he believed that, with dogs as draught animals, he had a good chance of succeeding. His departure certainly seemed to promise this as, with light loads, the dogs shot forward across the ice barrier, followed by the men on skis, who had attached themselves to the backs of the sledges by tow ropes. They picked up their supplies at the depot at latitude 80° and from there on laid a depot at every degree of latitude along the barrier, which ended at latitude 85°. Here they left a very large depot and took sixty days' supplies with them.

Although by this stage they had forty-two dogs with them, they expected to return with only twelve, planning to feed dog to dog along the route, in order to cut down the amount of dog-food needed. Ahead of them mountains blocked their path and they climbed to a height of 930 feet (283 metres) to camp. Between them and the Pole was a distance of 341 miles (548 kilometres).

At times they came to impassable areas of crevasses and had to climb as much as 2,000 feet (609 metres) to reconnoitre a route south. With chasms on one side of them and mountains on the other they had to take great care to avoid the avalanches crashing down the slopes.

In one ascent they climbed 5,750 feet (1,752 metres). The dogs were going well but Amundsen decided to sacrifice the twenty-four weakest ones. They were killed and some of them fed to their companions – appropriately enough, the camp was called the Butcher's Shop. Each man killed those of the doomed animals that belonged to his own team. The task was unpleasant, but as Amundsen argued, 'We had agreed to shrink from nothing in order to reach our goal.' Making a depot of the dog carcasses and other inessentials, they were about to leave when one of the men stuck an upright skistick by the side of the cairn. This spontaneous gesture was to save their lives.

So much travelling was done in poor visibility that there was a real danger that they might not find their way back. Monsters of crevasses lay waiting to swallow them up if they made a false move. They were thankful they were wearing skis, for without them they would certainly have broken through the frail snow bridges to the fathomless chasms beneath.

On leaving the mountainous area and approaching the polar plateau, they were held up for four days by a blinding storm. Although conditions were bad outside, the inactivity that was now forced on them, so near the Pole as it seemed, was unbearable, and on the fifth day they decided to brave the elements.

In the difficult areas, two men roped themselves together to reconnoitre a good route for the others, picking their way through a labyrinth of yawning chasms and deep abysses where a careless move could have meant death. They tacked and turned to find a way across enormous battlefields of jumbled ice, and for every mile gained in these confused areas they detoured ten.

During the journey 150 snow beacons were erected. In each of these was deposited a piece of paper giving the number and position of the beacon and indicating the distance and direction to be taken to reach the next beacon north. To begin with these cairns were placed every 15 kilometres (9 miles), but later at every fifth (third mile). It was this foresight that gave Amundsen his success. In territory as unfamiliar as this, through which they sometimes travelled in snow storms, no trouble was too much to ensure that they did not lose their way on the return.

In one area, which they called the Devil's Ballroom, they had an unusually unpleasant experience. They found themselves on an area of snowless glacier which sounded hollow beneath their feet. Suddenly some of the dogs broke through the apparently solid surface, hanging by their harnesses until they were pulled up. Beneath the top crust was a gap of three feet to the ice below – it did not look dangerous until one of the men fell through and found that the ice below was also a fragile crust. As he was disappearing through it he managed to grab onto a loop of rope attached to the sledge and haul himself to safety. There was no knowing how many layers of ice there were or what finally lay beneath, but when the men broke open the peculiar dome-shaped pieces scattered about the area, they found they were hollow inside, 'falling into black, bottomless pits'. After two narrow escapes, the party bade farewell to the Devil's Glacier as they called it, and began the last stretch of the outward journey to the Pole.

The first excitement on the polar plateau was the passing of Shackleton's farthest south, just over 100 miles (160 kilometres) from the Pole. With great emotion the Norwegian flag was hoisted on the leading sledge. From now on every inch of territory was unexplored by man. By now the five men were a sorry sight – their faces were badly frostbitten and the wounds were weeping sores. Despite the cold they were in good spirits and with no difficulty they covered an average of 20 miles (32 kilometres) a day.

On 13 December they had reached a latitude of 89°45'. Amundsen later remembered feeling as he had done when a little boy on Christmas Eve. The next day, 14 December 1911, a simultaneous 'Halt!' rang out from all the sledge drivers. By dead reckoning they had reached the Pole!

The men erected a tent to which they tied the Norwegian flag and a pennant with the name *Fram* written on it. Inside they left a letter to King Haakon VII of Norway which announced the victory. In a note addressed to Scott, Amundsen asked him to deliver the letter to the Norwegian King.

While Amundsen savoured his success, he could not help musing how strange it was that a man who wished so much to be the first at the North Pole should find himself instead at the South Pole. 'Can anything more topsy-turvy be imagined?' he asked.

On 17 December they left the Pole. Amundsen noticed with pleasure that 'the beacons shone like lighthouses in the sunlight'. At last they could turn their backs on the wind which had plagued their approach. They had plenty of food and plenty of time. Victory was behind them and they felt no inclination to extend their explorations further. The dogs covered 15 miles (24 kilometres) easily, and Amundsen took daily rests of up to sixteen hours. The delays tried the patience of everyone, but Amundsen appears to have been thinking of his promise to return on 25 January.

As he had expected, the landmarks on their return looked completely different from how they had remembered them, and they suffered some anxious moments before finding the meat they needed at the Butcher's Shop. It was only because someone noticed that upright ski sticking out of the snow that they were able to find the place.

Well fed and well rested, the ski runners raced ahead of the dog teams, skiing down the ice falls onto the Axel Heiberg Glacier like olympic athletes on a giant slalom.

In a few minutes they had descended 10,000 feet (3,000 metres). The return from there was without incident, and on 25 January, exactly as he had intended, Amundsen led his victorious party into Framheim – the name he had given his winter base.

While the Norwegians rejoiced, several hundred miles away, Scott and his companions starved. Beaten to the Pole, they had already begun their return journey which was to end in tragedy. Amundsen's words in reply to those who remarked that he was 'lucky' are worth remembering:

'Victory awaits him who has everything in order. Defeat is certain for him who has neglected to take the necessary precautions.'

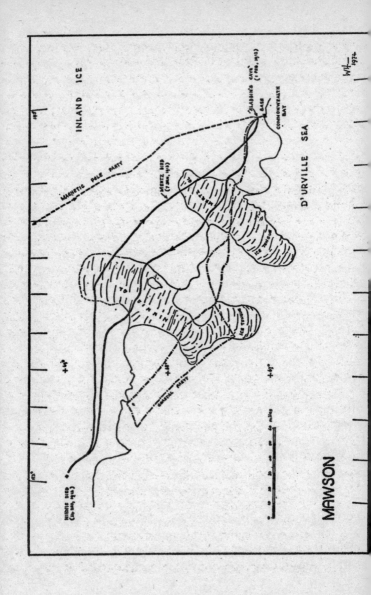

MAWSON

The windiest place on Earth: Mawson

One of the most remarkable scientific explorers to emerge in the Antarctic was Sir Douglas Mawson, an English-born Australian. He had accompanied Sir Ernest Shackleton to the Antarctic in 1907. Mawson had not joined Shackleton in his attempt to reach the South Pole but had stayed with the party led by Professor David which climbed Mount Erebus and located the South Magnetic Pole.

Mawson had great faith in the usefulness of exploration, believing that only with a full knowledge of every part of the earth could scientists offer a solution to the many problems which plagued mankind. He reasoned that with every advance of science there was a corresponding increase in the creature-comforts enjoyed by man, and he was convinced that the Antarctic might prove more valuable economically than was at first realized.

With these thoughts in mind, he organized an expedition in 1911, with the object of exploring the section of Antarctica which lay nearest to Australia, together with investigations of the ocean and sea-bed between Australia and the Antarctic. His idea was to establish several bases in the Antarctic which would be linked together by radio and he hoped that the meteorological data that could be gathered by his expedition would be invaluable to the shipping of Australia and New Zealand.

His hopes were well founded, and the geographical

achievements of his expedition were magnificent – over
three thousand miles of new territory were explored and
three scientific stations were established, of which two were
also wireless stations. Besides this, his studies of sea life
were remarkable. But it is only when we examine the appalling conditions in which his parties worked that we can
really judge the greatness of his achievement.

The area Mawson chose to explore is the windiest place
on earth. Hardly a day passes without a blizzard blowing.
Frequently hurricane winds last for weeks on end and gusts
as high as 200 miles (320 kilometres) per hour are not un-
common. While Mawson was there whirlwinds with a diameter of from a few to a hundred yards (metres) swept
through their camp, spiriting away objects lying in their
path. On one occasion he noted that a 'whirly' whisked the
lid of an air-tractor case, weighing more than three hundred-
weight (150 kilogrammes), right into the air and dropped it
fifty yards (45 metres) away. An hour later the lid was again
picked up by the wind and hurled back to its original position where it struck rocks with such force that it shattered.

It is not surprising that with winds of such intensity the
whole surrounding area was flattened. Mawson established
his base at Cape Denison on Adelie Land. He found a spot
sheltered by an upstanding rock on which to erect his hut.
From its door the men could look out at the terrifying sight
of gale-whipped seas, while to the back of the hut stretched
an unbroken plateau of ice with no feature to relieve its vast
monotony. So used did they become to the incessant howl
of the wind that on the few occasions when there was a lull
they found the silence so intense and eerie that they could
not sleep.

With winds fluctuating day after day from gale to hurricane force, they had to take great care to secure everything;
but even so, valuable articles were occasionally blown away.

Greater care had to be taken to make sure that the men themselves were not carried out to sea, and they soon developed a technique of moving about in blizzards.

Mawson describes the problems encountered on leaving the hut: 'The first difficulty was a smooth, slippery surface offering no grip for the feet. Stepping out of the shelter of the hut, one was apt to be immediately hurled at full length down-wind. No amount of exertion was of any avail unless a firm foothold had been secured. The strongest man, stepping onto ice or hard snow in plain leather or fur boots, would start sliding away with gradually increasing speed, in the space of a few seconds, or earlier, exchanging the vertical for the horizontal position. He would then either stop suddenly against a jutting point of ice, or glide along for twenty or thirty yards till he reached a patch of rocks or some rough sastrugi [snow chiselled by the wind].'*

They soon learnt never to go about without crampons on their feet, and in time they became masters of the art of walking into the wind. They had to lean forward so far that a sudden drop in the wind would send them sprawling on their faces. Before they had learnt this 'hurricane-walking', as Mawson described it, they often crawled about on all fours although the more inventive amongst them found they could travel with great success by sliding across the surface with a board under their knees.

The wind was hazard enough, but added to this was the blowing snow, which at times was so thick that objects three feet (one metre) away could not be seen. Its effect on a man was to send him gasping for breath inside the hut. It was a dreadful place, but the men bore it all with amazing cheerfulness. At times it was sheer torture to go outside to read the various scientific instruments scattered some distance

* Mawson, *Home of the Blizzard*

from the hut. Not only was the wind a factor they had to contend with, but the combination of wind and cold produced temperatures so chilling that to have been caught out for any length of time would have meant freezing to death.

Winter added another terror – days and nights of uninterrupted darkness when the instruments had still to be checked. To leave the warmth and cheerfulness of the hut was like entering a world full of malevolent spirits. Mawson describes how the men stumbled and struggled through the gloom while the merciless blasts of wind stabbed, buffeted and froze them, and while the stinging drift blinded and choked them.

Besides their scientific work they had to collect supplies of ice, and stores had to be brought in. The dogs needed to be cared for and the entrance kept free of drift. Always their faces became masked with ice while unseen hands appeared to clutch at their clothes, hacking and tugging with insane fury.

The effect of the snow particles which hurled through the air was apparent all round them, cutting through pillars of ice in a few days; and it 'frayed rope, etched wood and polished metal'.

On long journeys it was so difficult to pitch camp in the wind that the men had to hack shelters out of the ice. One such shelter was dug beneath the ice itself. A deep vertical trench opened into a room which they hewed out to a size large enough to shelter three men. They called it 'Aladdin's Cave' as the millions of ice crystals scintillated in the light, giving it a magical quality. Shelves were chipped out of the walls to house primus stoves, spirit bottles, matches and kerosene. In order to hang up a piece of their clothing, they used to moisten one corner and press it against the wall for a few seconds – it quickly froze and would remain hanging.

It was a very useful cave because the men did not need to

go outside to collect ice for their cooking; they just chipped away a block from the side. The rubbish they dropped down a crevasse nearby, and on clear days, light filtered in from above. A similar cave was made for the dogs, but unfortunately they sometimes froze to the ice and had to be chipped free.

Mawson set a programme for various parties to attempt while he and two others, Ninnis and Mertz, tackled a journey of exploration inland. To begin with they had agreed to rendezvous with various other parties in the area, but on 17 November, eight days after setting out, they moved eastwards on their own.

The going was hard over a surface so deeply eroded by wind that the sledges continually capsized into troughs. Each man took it in turn to run ahead, with the dogs guiding him, from ridge to ridge over the waves of snow. It was difficult to keep a footing and the men often fell and bruised themselves on the jagged ridges. When at last the surface did improve, Mertz put on skis and became the forward runner.

It was a nerve-racking journey. Sometimes they sledged over thin bridges of snow that concealed crevasses and on one occasion a team of dogs fell in and had to be hauled out, fortunately none the worse for the experience. Frequently they camped in an area of gaping holes which lead down into darkness, to a depth they could not guess.

There seemed no end to the obstacles in their paths. Some reached a height of 200 feet (60 metres) where glaciers had puckered and folded under tremendous pressure, and at other times there were precipitous falls of ice to be crossed and deep chasms to be avoided.

At one camp, at a height of 2,350 feet (620 metres) they were hit by a blizzard which buried the dogs and the sledges under a mound of drift. When they were dug out, snow was caked round the dogs' eyes and they had to scrape it away with their paws or rub their faces on the ground.

Men and sledges took a hammering and the third sledge was so badly damaged that they eventually discarded it. All the equipment was then divided amongst the remaining two sledges, with most of the food and the best dogs attached to the sledge second in line – the men reasoned that if a crevasse gave way then the first sledge, with the less important gear, would be lost, and not the vital one containing their food.

On 14 December the weather was good. The men of the party were pleased with the distance they had covered, and the new features they had recorded, but they had decided to sledge a bit further, to get within sight of Oates Land before beginning the return journey. Mertz, as usual, was skiing ahead and seemed in a happy frame of mind, singing to himself. After a while he paused and held up a skistick, which was a signal that there was something unusual to watch for. Mawson looked out for crevasses although it was unlikely that they would meet any on this stretch of hard, compacted snow. Seeing nothing alarming when he reached the place where Mertz had signalled, he jumped onto the sledge to do some work on his notes of the previous day. A moment later, glancing at the ground, he saw a faint indication of a crevasse. Although it did not look dangerous, he turned to warn Ninnis, who was on foot beside the second sledge.

Had Mawson not jumped onto the sledge when he did, he would certainly not have lived to tell his story. The irregularity in the surface was indeed the lid of a crevasse, and only by distributing his weight over a larger area, when he sat on the sledge, was he able to cross it without going through. Fate was not so kind to poor Ninnis.

Seconds after returning to his work, Mawson noticed that Mertz had stopped and was gazing anxiously past Mawson in the direction from which they had come. Turning to see what was the cause of his anxiety, he found only his own sledge tracks running back into the distance. Ninnis had vanished. Hastening back along his tracks, he came to a gaping hole in the surface – two sets of sledge tracks led up to it on the other side, but only one continued on his side of it.

Waving to Mertz to bring up some rope, Mawson leaned over the side of the crevasse and shouted into the black hole below. The only sound he heard was the moaning of a dog, lying on a ledge just visible 150 feet (45 metres) below. For three hours they called unceasingly, but no sound came back – the dog had ceased to moan and lay without movement.

A fishing line was lowered. It reached only to the ledge on which the dog lay. 'On either side the crevasse descended into blackness.' All the men's food except ten days' supply had gone, together with the tent and the best dogs. The men stood by in stunned silence.

The tragedy was enormous, and action seemed the only cure to their distress. They travelled to a high point nearby to complete their observations, and then made a thin soup for themselves by boiling all the old food bags. The dogs fared equally badly on worn-out fur mitts, fur boots and several spare raw-hide straps – they devoured the lot. After the meal, the men again called down the crevasse, in case their companion had been knocked unconscious by the fall and had recovered enough to answer, but there was no reply. They abandoned hope for their lost companion, and with a heavy heart Mawson read the burial service before turning for home.

With the tent gone, the men had to try and utilize the spare tent cover, and when they came to the camp where the third sledge had been discarded, Mertz set to work to build a frame to support the makeshift tent. There was just enough room when it was finished for two men to lie down, but there was no room to move about or to sit up.

The dogs they were left with were a miserable lot, and their condition was not made any better by lack of food. One by one they were killed and fed to the others – even the men had to eat the tough stringy flesh. It was now midsummer and the surface was not good for travelling during the day, so they travelled at night. Often they stumbled and slipped. The dogs that were too weak to walk were put on the sledge, which the men hauled, because they would need the meat when their sledging rations ran out. Christmas Day was celebrated by eating dog stew and dividing two scraps of biscuit found in a spare kitbag.

By New Year's Day Mertz was beginning to feel ill from eating dog meat. Mawson persuaded him to ride for a while on the sledge, but his condition deteriorated and he could not bear the intense cold. For two days they rested in the cramped little tent, where Mawson tried to comfort his wretched companion. But there was no hope for him; time was slipping by, and every delay meant less chance of Mawson surviving long enough to reach his base. But he would not desert his companion. On 7 January, Mertz became weak and helpless and after a long day in which he became delirious, talking incoherently, he died.

Mawson was himself by this time in a weak state. He was 100 miles (160 kilometres) from the hut, with little chance of reaching it. He hoped to be able to leave the records of the expedition and the diaries on some prominent place where they would be found by a search party. Hunger gnawed at his stomach and frostbite had attacked his toes, making them black and festering. It was a great temptation to stay in his sleeping bag and let death take him, but something made him fight on. With great effort he cut down the sledge to make it lighter and loaded it with the barest essentials; and then, piling snowblocks around Mertz and making a cross out of pieces of sledge, he prepared for the final test. For three days he was held up by bad weather, but he utilized the time by cooking all the dog meat and making a rough sail out of Mertz's Burberry jacket to put on the sledge. When he did set out alone on 11 January the weather was fine.

Mawson writes that from the start his feet felt lumpy and sore. They became so painful that after a mile of walking he had to stop to see what was causing the discomfort. The sight of his feet gave him quite a shock, 'for the thickened skin of the soles had separated in each case as a complete layer, and abundant watery fluid had escaped into the socks. The new skin underneath was very much abraded and raw'.

The best thing Mawson could think of was to smear the new skin with lanolin, and then to bandage the skin soles back into place. Over the bandages he wore six pairs of thick woollen socks, fur boots and a crampon overshoe of soft leather. Then, removing most of his clothing, he walked along letting the warm sun nurse his aching body.

Several days later, still alive, but weaker, he had a narrow escape when he fell through a snow-bridge into a crevasse. Fortunately, his harness, which was attached to the sledge, saved him. He had tied the rope to the sledge in such a way that should he fall in there would be a strong likelihood of the sledge bridging the gap. It did just this, and after dangling in space for several minutes, Mawson summoned enough strength to pull himself, inch by inch, up the rope and onto the overhanging snow-lid. Just as he was climbing out, a further section of the lid gave way and he felt himself plunging again, only to be halted with a backbreaking jolt at the end of the rope.

This time Mawson really felt the end had come. He was exhausted, weak and chilled. As he looked into the black chasm, the temptation to slip from his harness seemed the sweetest solution to the agony that faced him. But once again something made him think better of the idea, and, collecting all his strength for a final effort, he slowly drew himself again towards the surface. This time he emerged feet first, still holding the rope, until he had extended his full length on the solid snow. The strain of his exertions then overpowered him and he lay for an hour unable to move.

The prospect of similar accidents could not be overlooked, and Mawson decided to make a rope ladder out of a length of alpine rope which he attached both to himself and to his sledge. At least if it did happen again he would be able to climb out more easily – that was if the sledge did not fall down the crevasse too. He had occasion to thank his foresight when he twice pulled himself out of a crevasse by means of his makeshift ladder.

On 29 January Mawson came across a cairn left by a party of his men who had been there six hours before. He found a bag of food and a note stating that the ship had arrived at the hut and was waiting. He read that Amundsen had reached the Pole.

With plenty of food, Mawson soon became hopeful that he would reach the hut. Severe weather delayed him a week at Aladdin's Cave, which he reached on 1 February, but from there on there was no stopping him. As he covered the last 5 miles (8 kilometres) to the hut he could see the ship, a speck on the horizon. He was not left alone, however, because five men had stayed behind and a new wireless operator had been landed. As Mawson gazed at the receding ship he thought 'What matter!' The long journey was at an end – a terrible chapter of his life was finished.

Happily, many years of life stretched ahead of him, which he devoted to science and during which many people were to benefit by his inspiration.

Shipwreck:
Shackleton

'She's going, boys. Abandon ship! I think it's time to get off.' There was no panic as the exhausted men of the *Endurance* clambered over the splintering decks of the ship. No order was given to take to the boats, although these had been off-loaded, for all around the stricken ship was ice. Ten million tons of ice were pressing against her sides, staving in her planks two feet (600 millimetres) thick and buckling the steel floor-plates which screeched and clanked as they rubbed against each other. For days the groans of the besieged ship had haunted the air, making sleep impossible for the men dropping with fatigue. For three days the pumps had been manned unceasingly, in a desperate effort to stem the flood that invaded the ship – but the water turned to ice. Three times the floes on either side closed in while the vessel screamed under the strangling pressure. The men shuddered as they dragged their gear onto the ice, unable to look back at the vessel they were abandoning in her agony.

Whatever the relief to have escaped from the doomed ship, theirs was a terrifying plight. They were stranded on the icy wastes of the treacherous Weddell Sea in the Antarctic, halfway between the South Pole and the nearest outpost from which they could obtain help – some twelve hundred miles away.

On one man alone lay all the burden of responsibility.

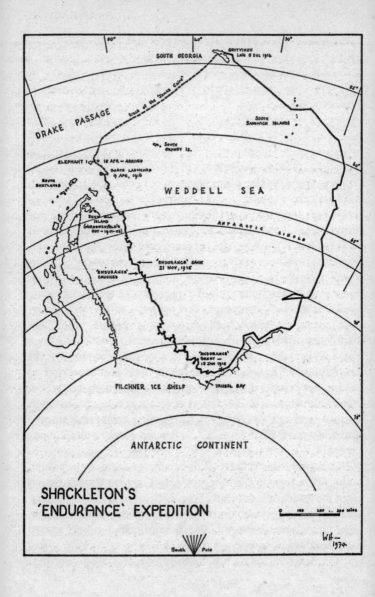

SHACKLETON'S
'ENDURANCE' EXPEDITION

Aloof from his twenty-seven men huddled in their tents, Sir Ernest Shackleton watched the pack for signs of danger. Tired though he was, he could not rest. Deep anxiety kept him on his guard. Suddenly, snake-like cracks raced through the ice towards the tents. Hurriedly Shackleton roused the men, who jumped, bewildered, to their feet. The order was given to move camp, and they stumbled headlong into the night, desperate to find safety on a larger floe.

Fortunately they did not have to travel far to find a suitable camp-site. The tents were erected and the exhausted men tumbled inside; some collapsed on ground-covers, others on the bare snow. So cold were they that they had to huddle against each other to keep from freezing in their sleep. In his own tent Shackleton confided to his diary: 'I pray God I can manage to get the whole party safe to civilization.'

For three weeks they could hear the groans of the beleaguered ship. Giant arms of ice broke through her sides and remained there, supporting the battered hull. She would remain on the ice until the pressure eased and, braving the risks, the men boarded her to get supplies. So great had been the pressure on the craft that she was warped along her entire length. During salvaging operations one day, ten emperor penguins waddled up to gaze at the stricken vessel. With one accord they raised their heads and let out piercing, dirge-like cries. The sound was so eerie and frightening that the men stopped in their tracks and one sailor blurted: 'Do you hear that? We'll none of us get back to our homes again.' It was only natural that anyone in those circumstances would have been quick to see an ominous sign in anything unexpected, but they must all have wondered the same thing when, on 21 November 1915, they watched the tortured ship finally sink.

*   *   *

Fifteen months before, the *Endurance* had left London in the command of Sir Ernest Shackleton, for an expedition which had as its objective a pioneering journey across the Antarctic continent. The expedition was to start from the coast of the Weddell Sea, cross the South Pole and to end at McMurdo Sound on the edge of the Ross Sea. The day the *Endurance* was due to sail, war broke out. The news put Shackleton in a dilemma. Four years he had worked, planning the Imperial Trans-Antarctic Expedition. Vast sums of money had been spent – all of which would have to be paid back if he did not go. Pride and patriotism had been the motives for organizing the expedition, and now pride and patriotism told him that he should fight for his country instead.

After much thought he mustered the crew to explain the situation, then, acting with their approval, he telegraphed the Admiralty offering to put the entire expedition at their disposal. Their answer was brief: 'Proceed'. A few hours later, Winston Churchill sent a longer telegram stating that the government wanted the expedition to go. Shackleton's dilemma was resolved.

At South Georgia, a whaling station and the last port of call, Shackleton heard the news that the ice in the Weddell Sea was worse than anyone could remember. He would have to try and avoid the centre of the pack and skirt round the ice to Vahsel Bay. A couple of weeks out of South Georgia in December 1914 they found themselves beset in what seemed 'a pudding of ice'. It was soft and slushy, eventually freezing them in. A freak northerly gale crowded the whole pack together and only a freak wind in the opposite direction could free them. But the Weddell Sea is not renowned for its winds, and as the sun set on the Antarctic winter, the expedition that had set out so confidently found itself marooned in a frozen desert of ice.

As leader of the expedition, Shackleton's duty was to keep the men happy, but alert for any emergency. They would need to be kept busy, but the work must be interesting. Competitions and festivities would have to be organized to lift the men's spirits and, above all, everything must be done to avoid the depressions that could develop if they were allowed to brood on the fearfulness of their situation. On previous expeditions, men had gone mad, so terrified were they by the isolation and the darkness.

A wire was put up around the ship on posts, and lights were fitted which shone onto the ice, to encourage the men to go for short walks. But even with all the distractions, the men longed for the arrival of the sun and some warmth, so that they could get on with their journey.

For nine months the ship was held fast by the ice, then in July it began to vibrate. For the first time the men sensed motion in the pack. Soon the movement increased as high winds screamed through the rigging and blasted the face of the pack. Cracks formed, ice jostled, and soon the whole gigantic ice cover was in motion. Floes collided with each other and built up into walls of jumbled ice. The ship began to creak and groan and as the ice began to squeeze it in, the men grew alarmed and jittery. When the water poured in, they worked frantically at the pumps; but by the time they abandoned ship, nothing further could be done to save the *Endurance*.

With the loss of the ship, any hope of making the pioneering journey across the southern continent sank. But more important now than any journey of exploration was the problem of how to get the men safely home.

Few could have accepted the burden of responsibility that fell upon Shackleton's shoulders. But he was no ordinary man. From his youth he had been a fighter. Pig-headed and obstinate under attack, he earned the respect of his fellows and superiors during his apprenticeship in the merchant navy. He had sailed for several years on tramp steamers to all corners of the world. He loved a challenge and hated routine. Poetic, afraid of nothing and endowed with inexhaustible energy, he was above all a leader.

Already, he was adored by the public. Flamboyant and courageous, he had won people's hearts by his daring explorations in Antarctica. After his first expedition to the south with Scott in 1902, he had organized an expedition on his own with the intention of reaching the South Pole and the South Magnetic Pole. A separate party on that expedition did in fact reach the Magnetic Pole, but the story of Shackleton's endeavour to reach the South Pole is one of such heroic achievement that he returned to England a national hero.

Shackleton had reached lat. 88°23' S, just 97 nautical miles (180 kilometres) from the Pole, when he turned back. He and his men were weak from shortage of food, from cold and from force-marching at such altitudes. (The South Pole is situated on a high plateau almost 10,000 feet [3,000 metres] above sea level.) He was within reach of the Pole but with a full team could not travel fast enough to make the food spin out. It was tempting to try it alone, but he had to think of his men. It was this concern for his men's lives, rather than for his own personal glory, that made him the great man he was. And it was concern such as this that inspired his men to follow him and to attempt the impossible.

Now, with the *Endurance* crushed beneath the ice, there was never a greater call for Shackleton to show what kind of a leader he was. Stranded in a desert of ice, what chance was there that they could survive ? There was no hope of rescue – no one to help them get out but themselves. However depressed Shackleton felt, he never let his men know the full extent of his anxiety. He explained the dangers and possibilities, and set himself to be calm; the men followed his example.

The nearest chance of finding food was from a cache left by a relief ship on tiny Paulet Island – 346 miles away to the north-west over the jostling ice pack. The stores had been left by a ship sent to rescue some Swedish men who had been shipwrecked. It was thought they might come in use in a future emergency. Ironically, it was Shackleton who had been commissioned to buy these stores twelve years ago and it was Shackleton who now needed them desperately.

Each man was assigned a duty in case of emergency – if escape had to be made across ice the sledge drivers would harness the dogs while the others broke camp and helped stow the gear. Meanwhile, the boats were strengthened and improved in case they found themselves surrounded by open water. Time soon began to drag although there were frequent excursions to get seal for both men and dogs to eat.

As summer advanced, it was stiflingly hot in the tents; and the surface became a quagmire of melted snow and rotting ice. Several attempts were made to move camp, but the labour was exhausting and slow, and the ice became so treacherous that they had to retreat.

The ice began to break up, food became scarce and four teams of dogs had to be shot to save the seal meat for the men. It was a misery lying in wet sleeping bags, and the men became edgy and depressed. Shackleton went to great lengths to smooth over any friction and he insisted on sharing the discomforts with his men – no one enjoyed special privileges. He believed that any trouble among the men might make them work less efficiently – and the consequences of this could mean the difference between life and death.

As Christmas approached and the New Year began, it became obvious to Shackleton that they would not be able to reach Paulet Island. The ice was too treacherous to cross and although the floe they were on was drifting, it was not drifting in the right direction.

By March they felt the swell of the ocean beneath the pack. The men were tantalized by the thought of the sea, but there was no sight of it to encourage them. Rations were low – tea and coffee were finished and there was little blubber to use as fuel to melt ice. The weather was bitter and the men kept to their sleeping bags to avoid the cold.

Their hopes now lay in reaching Clarence Island or Elephant Island. If they could not reach either of these islands they would be at the mercy of the Atlantic. On 9 April the boats were launched as the ice was cracking up all around them. Rowing was cold and cramping work and the men were glad to stop and camp on a floe. But during the night a crack opened up beneath one of the tents and one of the men fell into the water. It was only the quick thinking of Shackleton that saved him from a dreadful death. Heaving the struggling man out of the water, still in his sleeping bag, he just got him to safety before the crack closed up with shattering impact. Shackleton himself was nearly lost when the piece of floe he was standing on drifted away. He had just shepherded his men across a widening gap to another floe when he vanished into the darkness. Fortunately some of his men launched a boat and followed the direction of his voice.

When the ice got too rotten to be safe, they kept to the boats. On several occasions they were nearly swamped in huge seas. Great masses of ice were driven to the crests of the waves and held there for a while before dropping with an explosion of water into the troughs beneath. The sailors were wet through and frozen to the bone, starving, parched with thirst and seasick; the salt water stung their frost-bitten sores. They put up a grim struggle to keep the boats afloat. For hours on end they took turns rowing – the darkness only increasing the danger and adding to their fatigue. Shackleton never slept or relaxed but called regularly through the night to the other two boats. At last, weary and almost spent, the men found themselves near the cliffs of Elephant Island.

On 16 April, six months after abandoning their ship, the party landed. The place was alive with penguins but these migrated a few days later. Soon winter would set in. There was no time to be lost if help was to be fetched and on 24 April Shackleton set out for South Georgia on the *James Caird* with five men. Before he left he made sure the twenty or so remaining men were safely encamped. It was a pathetic group he left, their faces thin with cold and hunger, their eyes sunken and ringed with black.

Ahead of Shackleton lay one of the stormiest stretches of ocean in the world. Many ships had foundered in its heavy seas – what hope was there for the little boat manned by six weakened men? The boat had had a cover built over it but still it shipped gallons of water and the men were constantly baling. Rest was impossible as the boat plunged, knocking the men against the boulders used for ballast. It was cramped and dark below decks and very cold.

Besides the sea itself, a new danger threatened their boat as ice began to settle on it, growing thicker all the time. The increased weight made the boat sluggish and top-heavy, so that they were in constant fear of it capsizing. The spare oars were ditched, as were two of the fur sleeping bags to lessen the weight; and the men had to chop away at the ice while clinging precariously with the other hand to the bucking boat. At one moment they felt their time had come as a gigantic wave broke over the boat, almost drowning them in the surf. Nothing but frantic baling kept them from sinking, as the boat shuddered under the blow.

For fourteen days they suffered hardship, hunger and

cold, together with unbearable thirst towards the end of the trip when the water supply ran out. Even when they sighted South Georgia their troubles were not over. A hurricane nearly dashed them against the rocks; but after all storms there is a lull, and in the calm that followed they managed to row into King Haakon Bay. It was a deserted place full of jagged reefs and glaciers running into the sea. Their journey was not finished yet. To get help they would have to go overland to a whaling station on the other side of the island.

While three of the men made a temporary shelter, Shackleton and two others left them on 19 May to cross the mountainous country between them and the whaling station. Their journey took them up and down mountains, across precipices, through crevassed snow-fields and along glaciers. Wherever they could they slid down the icy slopes on their behinds, with the inevitable result that the seats of their pants were in tatters. They slept rough, without the comfort of sleeping bags, and though almost dropping with exhaustion they staggered on, knowing that men's lives depended on them. It was not surprising that when they did stumble into Stromness, after thirty-six hours of tortuous marching, their appearance scared the lives out of the first people they met.

On 20 May the other three were collected by whaling ship; but it was still some time before the men on Elephant Island could be picked up. Several attempts were made by ships sent by the Uruguayan and Chilean governments to penetrate the pack, after the failure of the first whaling boat to get through. Time was running out for his men, and Shackleton had to use all his powers of persuasion to convince the various governments to lend help. It was wartime and ships were scarce. However, one final attempt was arranged by the Chileans and miraculously on 30 August they got through.

For those on Elephant Island, help came just in time. In the last few weeks they had been close to starving. It was four and a half months since Shackleton had left them and there was hardly a man amongst them who believed their leader could have survived. However, when the relief ship was sighted they went nearly mad with excitement. And when Shackleton showed his familiar sturdy form a spontaneous cheer rang out. For the man who had braved countless dangers to save them was to all the castaways 'The greatest leader that ever came on God's earth – bar none.'

Antarctica today

With the crossing of Antarctica in 1958 by Sir Vivian Fuchs and Sir Edmund Hillary, the curtain was closed on a great era of exploration.

Today, there is not an acre of Antarctica that has not been photographed or mapped from the air. Desolate and inhospitable as that continent may be, it still attracts scientists from many nations. Locked in that great icecap is the secret of the world's climate for the last million years or more. By studying the various layers of ice, scientists can not only tell what happened in the past, but can get a fairly accurate picture of what is likely to happen in the future. Even a simple answer to the question of whether the icecap is growing or shrinking is of vital importance, because from this, climatologists can decide whether we are to expect another ice age shortly, or whether we can expect to see our coastal cities swamped at some future date. For we are told that if just a quarter of the ice in the Antarctic melted the sea levels throughout the world would rise 50 feet (15 metres). You can imagine what disastrous effects that would have on human life. But apart from questions like this, the Antarctic is a treasure trove of information for innumerable branches of science.

Antarctica has been described as a 'weather factory for the entire southern hemisphere' and so is of great importance to meteorologists. The waters surrounding Antarctica are the richest in marine life in the world and may well supply the greater part of the world's food when other resources have run dry. It is ironic that such a desolate, barren region should hold so much interest to scientists.

In 1957 twelve nations participated in an International Geophysical Year – a year in which a systematic scientific study was made of the continent. So successful was it that the countries involved decided to sign an agreement, called the Antarctic Treaty of 1959, by which it was agreed that 'the vast uninhabited wastes of Antarctica shall be used only for peaceful purposes'. It was proposed that 'Antarctica should be open to all nations to conduct scientific or other peaceful activities there. There shall be prohibited any measures of a military nature, such as the establishment of military bases and fortifications, the carrying out of military manoeuvres, as well as the testing of any type of weapons.'

Happily the agreement has never been violated, and today the continent is dotted with scientific stations from many nations. Never have so many nationalities worked in such close harmony. In a world where strife and distrust are commonplace, it seems a great pity that we cannot enlarge the experience gained in Antarctica – so that throughout the world, we could all work together for the greater good of mankind.

Piccolo True Adventure

Richard Garrett
Great Sea Mysteries (illus) 35p

A collection of fascinating stories of great oceans and
strange ships, master-spies and mutineers, sabotage and the
supernatural, the heroism of young Grace Darling, and the
never-ending mystery of the *Mary Celeste* . . .

Hoaxes and Swindles (illus) 20p

The man who bought the Eiffel Tower, the famous bluffs on
TV's programme Candid Camera, and the story of the
Piltdown Man are some of the items in this amusing
collection of true-life hoaxes and swindles

Narrow Squeaks! (illus) 35p

Fascinating real-life stories of people who have had truly
miraculous escapes, against all odds

True Tales of Detection (illus) 20p

An anthology of solved crimes from the murder of
Lord William Russell in 1840 to the Great Train Robbery
in 1963

Piccolo Book of Heroines (illus) 25p

From Boadicea to Angela Davis, this fascinating book gives
you the true stories of your favourite heroines, their battles,
sacrifices, adventures, romances and triumphs

More True Adventure from Piccolo

Frank Hatherley
Bushrangers Bold! (illus) 20p

True and thrilling stories of Australia's legendary outlaws

Carey Miller
Submarines! 20p

Hazardous missions, daring exploits and rescue operations are retold in this book of true submarine stories

Airships and Balloons 25p

Amazing tales of airships and balloons, from the one-man hot-air balloons of the eighteenth century to the huge hydrogen-filled Zeppelins of World War 1

You can buy these and other Piccolo books from booksellers and newsagents; or direct from the following address:
Pan Books, Cavaye Place, London SW10 9PG
Send purchase price plus 15p for the first book and 5p for each additional book, to allow for postage and packing

While every effort is made to keep prices low, it is sometimes necessary to increase prices at short notice. Pan Books reserve the right to show on covers new retail prices which may differ from those advertised in the text or elsewhere

Great Polar Adventures

Marie Herbert was born in Ireland, but from the age of six to eighteen she lived in Ceylon and India, where her father was a professor of Veterinary Science. She then spent three years at drama school in London, and afterwards taught speech and drama until she married polar explorer Wally Herbert in 1969. She tells the story of his expedition across the Arctic in this book.

She has also written *The Snow People*, published in Pan Books, which is about the year she spent with her husband and their daughter living in an Eskimo settlement.